ST. AUGUSTINE'S
Home School Enrichment Program

American Studies Supplement
For Primary, Lower, and Middle Schools

Dedicated to Our Lady
in her Immaculate Conception,
Patroness of the United States of America

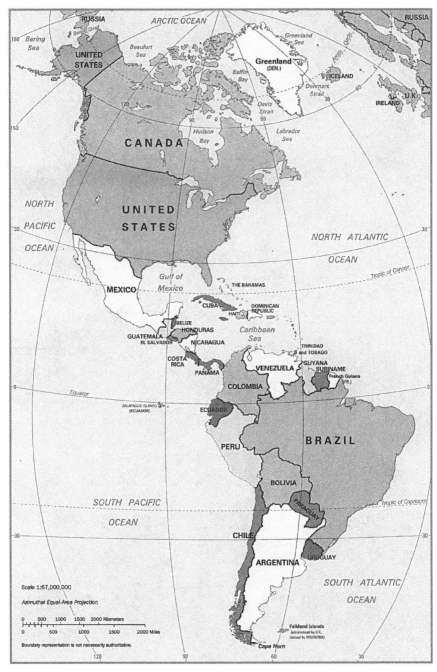

North America, Central America, and South America

Europe in the 18th century

The World—7 Continents and 5 Oceans

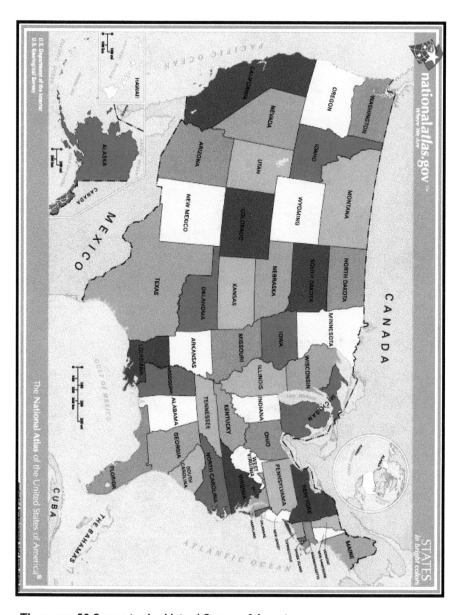

There are 50 States in the United States of America.

The Declaration of Independence was signed on July 4, 1776.

The Constitution of the United States was signed on September 17, 1787.

George Washington was our first President of the United States of America.

The Star-Spangled Banner

By Francis Scott Key

2. On the shore, dimly seen thro' the mists of the deep,
Where the foe's haughty host in dread silence reposes,
What is that which the breeze, o'er the towering steep,
As it fitfully blows, half conceals, half discloses?
Now it catches the gleam of the morning's first beam,
In full glory reflected now shines on the stream:
'Tis the star-spangled banner: oh, long may it wave
O'er the land of the free and the home of the brave!

3. Oh, thus be it e'er when free-men shall stand
Between their loved homes and the war's desolation;
Blest with vict'ry and peace, may the heav'n-rescued land
Praise the Pow'r that has made and preserved us a nation!
Then conquer we must, when our cause it is just;
And this be our motto: "In God is our trust!"
And the star-spangled banner in triumph shall wave
O'er the land of the free and the home of the brave!

The words of "The Star Spangled Banner" were written by Mr. Key in 1814 under stirring circumstances. He was detained on board one of the British ships which attacked Fort McHenry. All night the bombardment continued, indicating that the fort had not surrendered. Toward the morning the firing ceased, and Mr. Key awaited dawn in great suspense. When light came, he saw that "our flag was still there," and in the fervor of the moment he wrote the lines of our national song.

Christopher Columbus Discovers the New World for Spain

Ivan Aivazovsky, "The Disembarkation of Christopher Columbus with Companions"

1. He grew up in Genoa, Italy which was a trading city.
2. As a boy, he liked to play by the docks to hear the sailors' stories and he dreamed about sailing to distant lands one day. Geography was his favorite subject in school.
3. He became a sailor and dreamed of finding a new way to reach India and China by sailing west.
4. A Franciscan friar helped Columbus receive support

for his voyage from King Ferdinand and Queen Isabella of Spain.

5. His ships were called the *Nina,* the *Pinta,* and the *Santa Maria.* The *Santa Maria* was the biggest and was the leader, or flag-ship.

6. The Franciscan friar blessed the sailors before they left; they all went to Holy Mass before leaving.

7. When Columbus set out he was hopeful that (1) he would find a route to the Far East; (2) Spain would secure a rich trade; (3) there might be an opportunity to win souls for Christ. His name "Christopher" means "Christ-bearer."

8. Though it was a long and difficult journey, Columbus never lost courage. He was calm and brave, telling his men to "Sail on!"

9. In 1492, Christopher Columbus reached America, the New World. All the men offered thanks to God and claimed the land for the King and Queen of Spain.

10. He named the place *San Salvador* which means *Holy Savior.* This is an island in the Bahamas.

11. Although he didn't find any riches to bring back, he had made an incredible discovery: the New World.

The Spanish Conquistadors

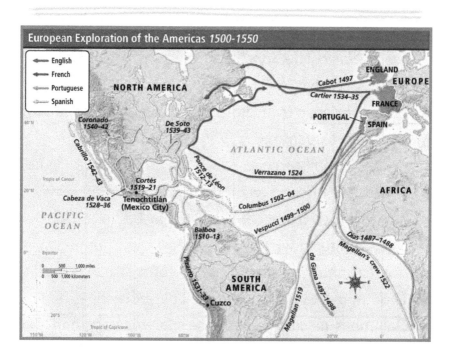

European Exploration of the Americas 1500-1550

1. **Hernando Cortes:** He was a Spanish soldier and conquistador who conquered the Aztec Empire in Mexico in 1521. Mexico became a part of New Spain.

2. **Francisco Pizarro**: He was a Spaniard conquistador who conquered the Incan Empire in Peru. Pizarro and other explorers claimed much of South America for Spain.

3. **Ferdinand De Soto**: He was a Spanish soldier who explored Florida and the Gulf of Mexico. His men discovered the mouth of the Mississippi River in 1541.

4. **Francisco Coronado**: He was a Spaniard who explored the southern United States in search for gold in 1540. One of his search parties didn't find gold, but they found the Grand Canyon of the Colorado River.

5. **Juan Ponce de Leon**: an adventurous Spaniard. He landed in Florida during Easter time of 1513. This is why he called it "Pascua Florida" or "Sunday of Flowers"

- The **Mayans** lived in the Yucatan and other parts of Mexico. They built cities with paved roads. They built temples on the top of huge pyramids. They wove beautiful cloth, fashioned jewelry, made books, pots and vases.

- The **Aztecs** conquered and enslaved the Mayans. They worshipped a god of war and made human sacrifices to the god to keep away his anger.

- The **Inca Empire** was in South America. They worshipped the sun and became great astronomers by studying the sun and stars. They were very good builders. They also had a strong government, with a system that helped those in need. Everyone shared the food they produced on their farm.

Soldiers and Saints

For a long, long time the people of Europe did not know about our land. They had never heard of the great Western continent.

They did not know about its high mountains, its great rivers, its rolling valleys, its wide plains. They did not know about its riches, its coal and oil, its iron and copper, its gold and silver.

The people of Europe had never heard of the beauty of the great Western continent. They had never seen its green forests, its purple hills, its blue lakes and streams.

They had never heard about its dry lands and its wet lands, its low lands and its high lands. They had never seen the bright-colored birds of the warm south. They had never seen the huge white bears of the cold north.

Then one day people from Europe, people from Spain, found our land. They found, at first, not the great Western continent, but a brave little island not far from its coast. They found other little islands. They called all these islands the Indies.

From the Indies the Spaniards sailed toward the west. They found the great Western continent. They found Florida. They found Mexico. They found South America.

Spain was a Catholic country. The king and queen were Catholics. The people, men and women, boys and girls, were Catholics. They wanted the Indies to be Catholic. They wanted the great Western continent to be Catholic.

Spain sent missionaries and soldiers to the new land. The soldiers carried the flag of Spain. The missionaries carried the cross of Christ. Franciscans came. Dominicans came. Jesuits came. They were brave and kind men. They came to win souls for Christ. The missionaries and soldiers of Spain climbed the high mountains of our land. They crossed the great rivers, the dry deserts, the wide plains.

They built towns and cities and forts. They gave them Spanish names: *Vera Cruz,* "True Cross"; *San Juan,* "Saint John"; *Santa Fe,* "Holy Faith."

One of the Spanish soldiers was Juan Ponce de Leon. In Spain he heard that there was gold in the New World. He set out from Spain to the islands of the west. He found no gold there, but he heard from the Indians a story about a fountain of water which made men young again when they drank of it.

There was not, of course, any such fountain; but Ponce de Leon went looking for it. He did not find it, but he found a beautiful place. The place, beside the Atlantic Ocean, was bright with flowers. Ponce de Leon found it on Easter Sunday, the day which the Spaniards call the Feast of the Flowers. He called the place *La Florida.* Today we call it Florida.

He found and tasted many springs. None of them made him any younger, but he liked the place so well that he went back to Spain for seeds, tools, horses, cows, pigs, and sheep. He brought these to start a new settlement. This was the first farming settlement in America. Ponce de Leon did not live long to enjoy it. He was wounded by an Indian arrow and died soon afterward.

Soldiers of Spain like Ponce de Leon made many

settlements, but most of these settlements did not last long. It was the missionaries of Spain who made the settlements which lived for a long, long time. Some of these settlements are still living, even though most of the missionaries died for their Faith.

In Kansas, in Florida; in New Mexico, and in Texas the early Spanish missionaries were put to death by the Indians. The missionaries gave their lives for the Faith. They were glad to die so that the Indian might know and love and serve God.

The missionaries built missions in the rolling valleys of our land. White buildings they were, with red roofs and square towers.

The missionaries, like the people of Spain, built the missions around a large open square. In the large open squares, which they called patios, they built fountains. They planted shade trees and gay colored flowers.

In the towers of the mission church they hung the bells which they had brought from Spain. The mission bells rang to call the Spaniards and the Indians to Mass, to Benediction, to evening prayer. On great feast days the bells called them to the joys of the feast, to music and dance and song.

By their brave and holy lives the priests of Spain brought Faith to the new country. On the mountains and in the valleys of the great Western continent the missionaries set the cross of Christ to save and bless our land.

Ships from Spain

Ships from Spain came sailing
Swiftly on the sea,
Bringing from the homeland
To the colony
Walnut trees and fig trees,
Grapefruit trees and cherries,
Orange trees and olive trees,
Hazelnuts and berries,
Horses, sheep, and cattle,
Peppers, oil, and cheese,
Spices, herbs, and lemons,
Honey from the bees.

Ships from Spain came sailing
Swiftly on the sea,
Bringing for the feast days
Of the colony
Tambourines and bagpipes,
Castanets and fiddles,
Kettledrums and trumpets,
Puppet shows and riddles,
Fireworks for the evening,
Songs for girls to sing,
Silver bells and gold bells
For the boys to ring.

Ships from Spain came sailing,
Swiftly on the sea,
Bringing best of all gifts
To the colony,
Priests who brought the Gospel

Of the Living Word,
Priests who taught the glory
Of the risen Lord,
Priests who lifted crosses
High above the sod,
Priests who lived, priests who died,
For our Land and God.

In 1492, Christopher Columbus discovered the "New World" for Europe.

5 Reasons for European Exploration:

1. To find the Northwest Passage
2. To find gold, silver, other valuables
3. To claim new land
4. To convert others to Christianity
5. For adventure

Our Lady of Guadalupe
Appears in Mexico in December, 1531

The Spanish victory over the Aztecs, brought an opportunity for the missionaries to bring the Catholic Faith and peace to the people living in darkness and fear.

Ten years later, the Blessed Virgin chose to appear before an Aztec Indian named Juan Diego to give a special message of compassion and piety to her children. She was shown to be the best apostle yet as thousands of natives converted each day after her apparitions and miracles. By the end of Juan Diego's life, the majority of Mexico had become Catholic.

Cortes had led the conquest of the Aztec Empire, but our Lady led the conquest of souls. Her apparitions initiated a tidal wave of conversions in the New World, and therefore is perhaps the most significant event in the history of the Americas, and certainly of the Church in America.

Carlos' Stories from Mexico
By Betsy Warren

Carlos moved to Honey Spring Valley from a country called Mexico. For hours he would sit under his big hat, which he called a sombrero, telling stories about his friends in Mexico.

Beto's Many Sombreros

For many months Carlos' friend Beto had wanted a new sombrero. Every day he thought about what it would be like. For one thing, it would be black with many bright colors on it. It would have a wide brim with little colored balls hanging down along the edge.

When Beto told his mother about his wish, she said, "You already have many sombreros, little Beto. Why would you want another?" Even as she said this she turned her head and smiled. She already knew why.

"The new one would be for the great feast day," replied Beto. "For the first time in my life, I will be going to the festival with you and Papa."

Papa was listening as he ate his breakfast. "Little boys must earn new sombreros," he said.

"How can I do that?" asked Beto. "In a family, when a boy does his work well, perhaps he can earn his wish. Who knows?" said Papa, shrugging his shoulders. "Now it is time for a boy called Beto to feed the turkeys and chickens and to gather the eggs."

Beto sighed as he walked over to the wall where his sombreros were hanging. l He took an old straw one from the wall and put it on his head. It was dirty and tom at the edges. When Beto leaned over to feed the chickens, one of them reached for a straw in his old sombrero, thinking it was a piece of hay.

Beto found so many eggs that he had to carry them in his sombrero to the house, making three trips.

"This sombrero is good for carrying eggs, but it will never do to wear to the festival," Beto told his mother. "It's too old and torn."

"That is so," replied his mother, "but perhaps even a very old sombrero may help a boy to get his wish. Who knows?"

Soon it was time for Beto to get out the little gray burro and to go off to the market with the eggs.

"My small sombrero with the wide red band is the one I shall wear to the market," said Beto as he hung the old straw one back on the wall.

Papa helped Beto load the eggs in the baskets that hung on the little burro's sides. Then Beto jumped on the burro's back.

"Get a good price for the eggs, and remember to buy all the things Mama told you to get," said Papa. "Don't be slow about getting back for lunch."

After Beto sold all of his eggs, he bought the colorful beads and the buttons that Mama wanted. He wanted very much to visit the place where sombreros were sold, but it was getting late so he rode back home, wearing his small sombrero with the wide red band on it.

"This is a fine sombrero for going to market," he told his mother when he got home, "but it is too small to wear to the festival. " "That is so," his mother agreed, "but perhaps even a very small sombrero may help a young boy to get his wish. Who knows?"

After Beto had eaten his lunch, Mama said, "It is too warm to work. It is time now to take a nap." Beto put on his biggest sombrero and started out to take a nap under a tree. "This is a fine sombrero to wear for a nap," he told his mother. "It is big and keeps the sun off my face, but it is too big to wear to the festival. It would bump into all the dancers."

After supper that evening, Papa said to Beto, "Your mother and I are going to take some eggs to our neighbors. You must stay here in case the coyotes come to rob us of our turkeys and chickens." Beto sat down by the door, watching his parents go down the road with a basket of eggs. Everything was quiet. The sun was just going down in the sky. The chickens and turkeys had flown up into the trees for the night.

Things were not quiet for very long. Soon the screaming and crying of a band of coyotes rang through the clear air. The sound came closer and closer. The chickens and turkeys moved arotlnd uneasily. "What shall I do?" Beto thought. As he picked up a big stick, a thought suddenly came to him. He ran into the house and got all of his sombreros from the wall where they hung.

He turned on the lamp and put one of his sombreros in each of the windows. He put the tallest one on his head and began to march beside the house like a soldier with the stick over his shoulder. Then louder and louder screamed the coyotes. Nearer and nearer they came. Faster and faster beat Beto's heart.

"What if the coyotes carry off our turkeys and

chickens," Beto thought. "Then there will be no eggs to sell and I will not earn a new sombrero."

Suddenly everything became very quiet. Beta could see the coyotes standing still and looking toward the house. "I think I have tricked them," he said to himself. "They think there is a person under each sombrero and that I am a tall man with a gun."

Sure enough, the coyotes suddenly turned and ran in the other direction as fast as they could. Just then Beto's mama and papa came home. "Oh, Beto! Beto!" they called. "Did the coyotes take our chickens and turkeys? We heard them screaming, but we could not get here any faster."

Papa and Mama smiled when they heard what Beto had done. "My sombreros helped me to gather the eggs, to go to the market, and to take a nap," the boy said. "Now they have helped me in another way. All the coyotes ran because they saw so many sombreros."

"Now you need one more sombrero -one that will help you dance at the festival," said Papa. "We will sell some eggs and one or two of the chickens and turkeys that you saved from the coyotes. Perhaps there will be enough money to buy the very sombrero you want. Who knows?"

Mama smiled at Beto and said, "Your many sombreros have helped you find a way to get your wish." The next week Beto danced at the festival wearing a new black sombrero with many bright colors on it and many little colored balls that hung down around the edges.

Our Lady and the Indian
on a Mountainside in Mexico

One morning when Carlos went to Confirmation
class at Holy Cross Church, Father Dale gave him a
special holy picture. It showed our Blessed Mother
dressed in colorful clothes and an Indian kneeling in
front of her. The other children wanted to know about
the picture, and so Father Dale told them this true
story that happened in Mexico many years ago.

One cold winter morning a poor Indian awakened
before sunrise and left his little village. He started off
for Mexico City, which was miles away. The old Indian's
name was Juan, which means John. He was a very
good Catholic, and he loved the Blessed Virgin in a
special way. On this morning Juan wanted to hear
Mass in honor of the Mother of God. Since there was
no church in his own village, he decided to walk all the
way to Mexico City.

As the old man walked along, a large, white cloud
seemed to be floating down the mountainside toward
him. Juan stood still and looked at the sight. He heard
a sweet voice calling his name. Juan hurried up the
mountain.

When he climbed nearer the strange sight, a bright
light shone through the cloud. Then something
wonderful happened. A very beautiful Lady appeared in
the cloud. "Juan, come closer," she said. When Juan
stepped closer, the lovely Lady said, "I am the Mother
of God. I want you to go to the bishop of Mexico and
tell him to build a church in this place in my honor.

Kneeling before the beautiful Lady, Juan watched her

disappear. Then he hurried on toward the city to do as she had asked. When he reached Mexico City, he went straight to the bishop's house and described what had happened.

Of course, the bishop found it hard to believe Juan, for he thought the poor Indian only imagined that he had seen the Blessed Virgin. The bishop told Juan that if our Blessed Mother really wanted a church built, she herself would have to give a sign from heaven.

The poor Indian started home feeling very sad. When he walked down the mountain, the Blessed Virgin appeared again in gleaming robes. Juan was happy to see the lovely Lady again, but he felt ashamed to tell her what the bishop had said. "No one will listen to me," Juan said. "I am only a poor Indian. The bishop thinks I only imagined that I saw you." Our Blessed Mother smiled at him. "Do not worry," she said. "Tell the bishop again that God wants a church built here in my honor."

You can imagine how afraid Juan was to return to the bishop, but he did exactly as Our Lady had told him. Again the bishop only smiled and said, "We should like to build a church in Mary's honor, but how can we know that what you claim is true unless we are given a sign from heaven?" The Indian left when he heard these words.

As he walked slowly down the mountain, two of the bishop's servants followed him. The bishop had sent them to watch Juan and to see if the Blessed Virgin really appeared to him. For a long while the servants followed Juan. Then suddenly he disappeared right before their eyes. In the meantime the Blessed Virgin appeared again to the Indian. "Do not worry," she told him. "Come here again tomorrow, and you shall have the sign the bishop wishes."

The Sign

When Juan reached home that night, he found his uncle very ill. He was afraid to leave the sick man and stayed, kneeling at his bedside all through the night and all the next day. Very early the following morning, just at daybreak, Juan thought his uncle was going to die. He decided to run to the city and get the priest. Then he remembered that he had not done as the Blessed Virgin had told him.

He started up the mountain worrying about it when suddenly Our Lady appeared again. Juan fell at her feet, bowed his head, and told her about his sick uncle.

"Do not fear," said the holy Mother of God. At this very moment your uncle is well again. You will not have to hurry for a priest." Then our Blessed Lady said something which surprised Juan. "I want you to go to the top of this mountain and pick the roses you will find there," she said. "Put them into your cloak, and return here to me." Now, never before had anyone seen roses blooming up on this mountain during the cold season. "How could roses bloom in winter?" the Indian wondered, but he obeyed anyway and went to look for the roses.

Juan had a pleasant surprise when he reached the top of the mountain. There he found the most beautifully shaped roses in full bloom. Very quickly he picked the roses, put them into his cloak, and hurried back to the Virgin.

Our Blessed Lady put her lovely hands over the roses as if she were blessing them. "Go now," she said. "Take these to the bishop. Tell him it is the sign for which he asked. Do not open your cloak until you see the bishop." Now, the poor Indian was happy as he hurried to the bishop's palace. When he got there, the servants wondered why Juan had his cloak wrapped around him. "What are you trying to hide in your cloak?" they asked. Juan remembered what Mary had told him. He wrapped the cloak more tightly around himself to hide the roses.

When the bishop finally came in, Juan exclaimed happily, "Here is the sign you asked for Our Blessed Mother has told me to bring it to you." As Juan unwrapped his cloak the beautiful roses dropped to the floor. The bishop was surprised and also a bit frightened when he saw the beautiful roses. He had a still greater surprise when he looked up and saw another wonderful sight.

There on Juan's poor cloak was a most beautiful picture of the Blessed Virgin. The bishop called all his servants into the room. They all knelt down and gave glory to God and His holy Mother.

The picture of Our Lady on Juan's cloak was hung in the largest church in Mexico City until the people built a new church in Mary's honor. The church that the Blessed Virgin asked to have built is still standing near Mexico City. People from all over Mexico go there on Mary's special feast day

Missionary Heroes in New Spain

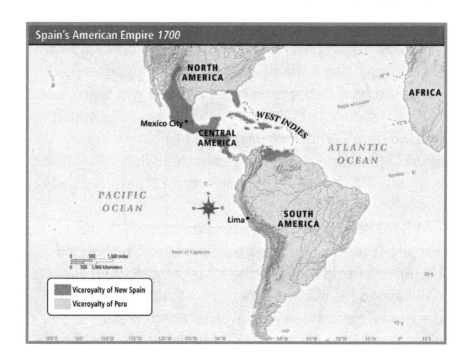

Spain's American Empire *1700*

NORTH AMERICA

AFRICA

Mexico City

WEST INDIES

CENTRAL AMERICA

ATLANTIC OCEAN

PACIFIC OCEAN

Lima

SOUTH AMERICA

Viceroyalty of New Spain
Viceroyalty of Peru

Many priests and missionaries came to the New World to teach the natives about Christianity. Some Indians were not friendly towards the Europeans. Many missionaries knew that they risked their life to try to become friends with the Indians and to teach them about Christianity. Many were killed for the Faith; these men and women who give their lives up for Christ are called "martyrs."

In the southwest, many Indians were friendly and the priests built missions for them. A mission had many things to help the Indians live in a better way: a school, workshops, a farm, cattle ranges, homes for the Indians and Priests, and most importantly it had a church, beautifully decorated with pictures and statues.

In South America

Two saints lived during the 17th century in Lima, Peru.

St. Rose of Lima, even from a young age, wanted to dedicate her life completely living for God. She started running a home for homeless children, elderly, and the sick. She practiced many corporal works and spiritual works of mercy, always practicing virtues with humility. She died when she was 31 years old and the whole city attended her funeral.

St. Martin de Porres grew up as a young boy in great poverty. His father had abandoned the family and Martin helped his mother support the family as a barber and give people different medical treatment. When he grew up, he became a Dominican brother. Brother Martin did many works of charity. He took care of slaves, the sick, and abandoned or orphaned children.

St. Peter Claver was from a rich family in Spain. He had many comforts and entertainments of life but he desired to serve God with his life instead. He joined the Jesuits and became a priest. Soon, he was sent to South America to be a missionary. There he worked among the Indians and the slaves. He would try to help the very poorest first. The slaves were treated terribly and so Father Claver would go and be with them, to give them love and care. While he treated their bodies, he also taught them about the Faith and about God's love for them. Most of the slaves in his town became Catholic because of his great example. Many people treated the slaves and Indians better because of Father Claver's example.

South America

I am the Atlantic Ocean

I am the Atlantic Ocean.
I join hot lands and cold lands.
I join high lands and low lands, wet lands and dry lands.
I join old lands and new lands.
I brought the ships of Columbus.
I brought the explorers and the missionaries.
I brought people from every country in Europe.
I brought people who wanted homes.
I brought people who wanted freedom.
I brought people who wanted to work, to learn, to pray, to love God.
I brought the Faith of the Old World to the New.
I brought the story of Christ, the love of Christ.
I am the Atlantic Ocean. I came from the hand of God.
He made me for the use of His children.
Sometimes storms break over me. Sometimes the sun shines brightly upon me. Sometimes I weep.
Sometimes I laugh. Always, everyday, I give glory to the God Who made me.

French Explorers and New France

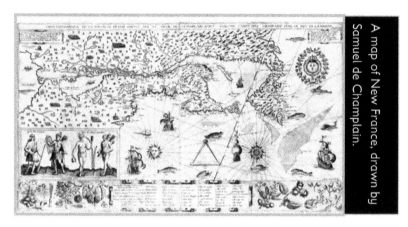

A map of New France, drawn by Samuel de Champlain.

At this time, Spain, England, and France were great rivals. France and England were eager to send explorers and colonists to North America.

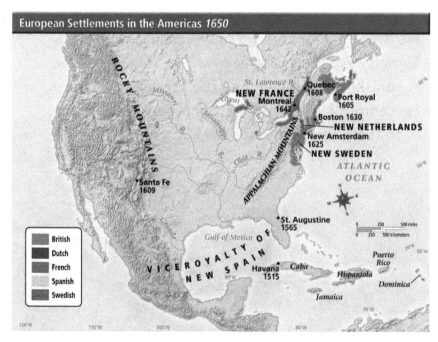

European Settlements in the Americas *1650*

Jacques Cartier (1535)

1. He was sent by the King of France to look for a passage across North America. He found a large body of water and called it the Gulf of St. Lawrence.
2. In his second voyage, he discovered a river flowing into the Gulf and called it the St. Lawrence River.
3. He discovered many Indian villages, such as one on an island. Because it had a great hill, Jacques Cartier called it Montreal "Royal Mountain."
4. From his discoveries, France was able to claim the St. Lawrence Valley.
5. 75 years later, France started building settlements in New France.

Samuel Champlain (1603)

1. He continued the explorations that Cartier began.
2. In 1608, he started the first permanent French settlement in the New World at Quebec.
3. Quebec was an important settlement for the fur trade. The Indians would trap animals and collect the furs for trade with the French. The furs were sold at a high price in France.
4. He became a friend with the Huron and Algonquin Indians. The Iroquois Indians were very hostile and violent against the French settlers.
5. During his exploration he discovered some very large lakes: Lake Champlain, Lake Huron, and Lake Ontario. These became a very important discovery to make travel easier through the chain of water "highways."

Trees

By Bliss Carman

In the Garden of Eden, planted by God,
There were goodly trees in the springing sod,-

Trees of beauty and height and grace,
To stand in splendor before his face.

Apple and hickory, ash and pear,
Oak and beech and the tulip rare,

The trembling aspen, the noble pine,
The sweeping elm by the river line;

Trees for the birds to build and sing,
And the lilac tree for a joy in spring;

Trees to turn at the frosty call
And carpet the ground for the Lord's footfall;

Trees for fruitage and fire and shade,
Trees for the cunning builder's trade;

He made them of every
grain and girth,
For the use of man in
the Garden of Earth.

Then lest the soul
should not lift her eyes
From the gift to the
Giver of Paradise,

On the crown of a hill,
for all to see,
God planted a scarlet
maple tree.

The Canadian Pioneers
By Fr. Hugh Sharkey

This was, in days gone by, a wilderness,
    Dense-timbered hills and plains of rocky soil.
Behold, the far-flung dwellings of a nation
    Rise-monuments to human hand and toil.

Honor to them-the noble pioneers-
    Planting a country's flag on unknown sod,
Bearing aloft the crucifix of Christ
    To teach to savage men the love of God.

Day after day they toiled with ready zeal
    To fell the forest and to till the sod,
And set aside in simple faith a day
    When they would rest and give their thanks to God,

Who looked with pleasure on their frugal life,
    Blessed with His love their every, little way,
Ripened with sun and rain their growing fields,
    Smiled down upon the little ones at play.

No monument arises to their name,
    No testimony written by our hand;
Only, where once a wilderness had stood,
    Behold-the far-flung nations of the land.

The Missionaries of New France

Blessed Bishop Laval: He was the first bishop of Quebec in 1658. At this time, his diocese was the entire area of New France. From a young age, his greatest desire was to become a missionary.

The arrival of the Ursuline Sisters.

When he became the bishop, he humbly started his work as leader and shepherd to the people in New France. He traveled by foot and canoe throughout his large diocese to serve his people and giving them the Sacraments. He fostered many good devotions within his diocese: special devotion to the Immaculate Conception, St. Anne, the Holy Angels, and the Holy Family. When the colonists treated the Indians unfairly, he bravely defended them. He invited many religious orders to help him with his work in the parishes, seminaries, schools, and hospitals.

PORTRAIT OF LAVAL, FIRST CANADIAN BISHOP.

St. Marie of New France: she was a widow at a young age and later joined the Ursuline sisters who asked her "to create a house for Jesus and Mary" in Canada. She organized the building of a small monastery and school for Indian and French girls. It also became a charitable house where anyone could find counsel and help if they needed. She also wrote dictionaries, catechisms, and prayer books in 4 different Indian languages.

The **Ursuline Sisters** came to New France in **1639**.

North American Martyrs

The Jesuits were the first priests to come from France to tell the Indians about Christianity. They first started preaching to the Hurons. These Indians were very friendly and welcomed the French priests.

These priests soon became known as "the Black Robes" because of their black habit. They first had to learn the Huron language, then started helping the sick with medicine and care. After spending some time with them, the priests began teaching the Indians about God and the truths of the Faith.

One of the priests was **St. Isaac Jogues**. After preaching to the Indians, he went to become friends with the Iroquois, but they took him prisoner and tortured him. He escaped with the help of kind men, but quickly returned to try to make friends with the Iroquois again and to tell them about God and heaven. He was captured again and was martyred. At this time, there were 7 other Jesuits killed by the Indians. They are all martyrs for the Faith. There is a shrine for these martyrs in New York.

St. Kateri Tekakwitha: She was a Mohawk Indian, born in the village where Father Isaac Jogues was martyred. Her mother and father died from small pox when she was only 4 years old. Her mother was a Christian and taught her about God before she died. Kateri converted when she was a teenager, although her uncle and other Indians persecuted her. Kateri wanted to dedicate her life to God and remain unmarried, offering her life to Jesus. She moved to a Christian village a few years later and was known for her charity, gentleness, and good humor. She died when she was only 24 years old.

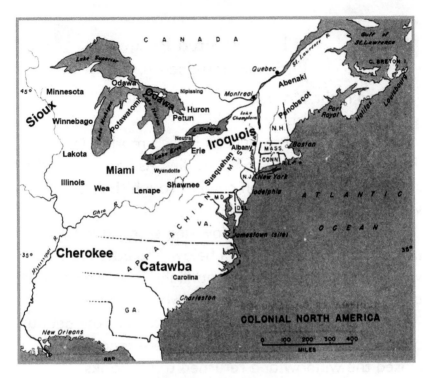

COLONIAL NORTH AMERICA

Indian Children
By Annette Wynne

Where we walk to school each day
Indian children used to play
All about our native land,
Where the shops and houses stand.
And the trees were very tall,
And there were no streets at all,
Not a church and not a steeple
Only woods and Indian people.
Only wigwams on the ground,
And at night bears prowling round
What a different place today
Where we live and work and play!

The Answered Prayer
By Sister Mary Henry, O.P.

"Good night, Mother!"

"Good night, Isaac!"

The door closed softly, and Isaac's mother left him. The boy turned back to his studies. As he worked, the soft spring breeze which came through the open window made his candle flicker.

He rose to shut the window and stopped for a minute to look at the town below. The little French village lay sleeping in the moonlight. The steeple of the church seemed to be tipped in silver.

The boy wished he could stay to admire the beauty, but both his time and the candle were precious. He closed the window and returned to his books.

As time passed, the candle burned low. When his lessons were ready for the next day, Isaac blew out the light and knelt to say his prayers. He held a little wooden crucifix in his hands and often bent to kiss the Sacred Wounds.

Isaac Jogues prayed with all his heart, "Oh, my God! How much You suffered for our souls! Dear Jesus, teach me how to suffer for You. Take my soul, my hands, my head, and my heart for Your work!"

Isaac Jogues was in many ways like other boys of his age, but in one way he was very different. He had a secret wish, which only his mother knew. He wanted to be a missionary. His goal was to travel to North America to teach the Indians about God. He knew that a missionary must be brave and kind and able to stand great hardships, and so he tried to train himself for this in his daily life.

The years passed quickly. Isaac became a Jesuit priest, and at last the day came when he was to offer his First Holy Mass. How happy his mother was to receive Holy Communion from her son's hands! But the good woman was sad, too, for she had learned that her son was to sail at once far, far across the sea, to the Jesuit mission in North America.

Father Jogues wrote a letter to his mother once each year from the New World. In his first letter he told her about the journey to the mission where he was to stay until he had learned the languages of the Huron Indians.

At this time there were only twenty priests to work among thirty thousand Huron Indians. On the journey to the mission, Father Jogues met with many hardships. He had to sit for hours in the canoe without moving. Mush, unsalted and without sugar, was the only food. At night he slept on the hard ground or on the rocky shore.

The Huron mission was called St. Joseph's. Here the missionaries lived in a bark-covered house with an opening in the roof to serve as a chimney and as a window. When it was closed at night, the smoke filled the house and made their eyes ache.

There was much sickness among the Indians, and many children died. The priests tried to baptize all of these little ones. Long afterward it was a comfort to Father Jogues to recall how many of these souls he had helped to reach heaven.

It was a good thing that Father Jogues knew how to

study because the Huron language is very difficult. He learned it at last and was then able to begin his work of visiting and teaching the Indians.

One day, when he was traveling through the forest with a group of Christian Indians and a couple of young Frenchmen, the party was attacked by a band of Iroquois Indians. French traders had fought the Iroquois, and from that day the Iroquois had been the enemies of the French. The priest could have escaped, but he stayed to help the young Frenchmen and was taken prisoner.

Father Jogues was beaten and tortured. His fingers were torn, and a spear was run through the palms of his hands. He was dragged from one Indian village to another. He suffered from cold, and most of the time he was hungry.

Through all that time, the good priest prayed. When the Indians made him run between two lines of warriors who beat him with clubs, he prayed. He called the lines of cruel Indian warriors "the narrow road to Heaven."

For months the Iroquois held Father Jogues prisoner. As he went through the woods he carved the Sign of the Cross and the name of Jesus upon the trees. He made many efforts to win the cruel Indians for Christ, but they would not even listen to the holy priest.

At last the prisoner was brought to a Dutch settlement in what is now the state of New York. Kindhearted people heard of the sufferings of the French priest and found a way to help him to escape to a boat in the Hudson River.

After a long and dangerous journey, Father Jogues reached the French coast. Dressed in rags, weak and ill from the hardships he had suffered, he made his way on foot to a Jesuit school. His Jesuit brothers did not recognize him when he knocked at the gates, but they took him in. When they heard that he came from the New World, they asked, "Do you know Father Isaac Jogues?"

"I am he," he answered humbly.

That night was a night of joy and thanksgiving in the Jesuit school.

The next spring, Father Jogues was happy to be sent again to his Indians in the New World. He lived there in great danger for several years, visiting many parts of the country and helping traders as well as Indians.

Once again he was taken prisoner by the Iroquois and held as a slave for a long time. He was beaten and wounded and suffered much until one day an angry Indian killed him.

The work of Saint Isaac Jogues was done. God had heard the prayer of the little boy who had once asked Him to take his soul, his hands, his heart, and his head to do His work on earth.

Knowest Thou Isaac Jogues?
By Francis W. Grey

A wayworn pilgrim from a distant shore
    Knocked at the convent gate at early day,
    Then waited patiently: "Whence com'st thou, pray?"
The brother asked. "From Canada"; the door
Was opened wide in welcome; faint and sore
    With many a toil he seemed, and long the way
    That he had journeyed; greatly marveled they
To see the cruel wounds and the scars he bore.

"Com'st thou from Canada?" the Rector said,
    Vested was he for Mass, yet came to see
The traveled guest, who answered, "Yes"; they led
    To welcome food and rest; then asked, "Maybe
Thou knowest Isaac Jogues? " He bowed his head,
    As one who shunneth honor-"I am he."

William Guy "Cauterskill Falls on the Catskill Mountains"

French Explorers of the "Great Water"

The course and watershed of the **Mississippi River** *The Father of Waters*

200 Miles
400 Km

Alberta · Saskatchewan · Montana · North Dakota · South Dakota · Wyoming · Minneapolis · Minnesota · Iowa · Nebraska · Kansas · St. Louis · Oklahoma · New Mexico · Red · Texas · Gulf of Mexico · New York · Pennsylvania · Ohio · Indiana · West Virginia · Kentucky · North Carolina

Father Jacques Marquette

1. He was a Jesuit missionary priest from France – sent to Quebec and learned some Indian languages to preach to them
2. He founded a mission for the Huron Indians at the city called St. Ignatius.
3. He learned about a Great River from the Indians; they called it "Father of Waters" or the "Great Water."
4. He understood the Indians and their customs, loved them, and won their respect.

41

5. His friend Louis Joliet and Fr. Marquette received a commission from the King of France to explore the "Father of Waters" or now known as the Mississippi River.
6. Exploration Route: Lake Michigan - Fox River – Wisconsin River – Mississippi River (he called it the River of the Immaculate Conception)
7. Journey home: Mississippi River – Illinois River – Lake Michigan

Statue of Fr. Marquette in the Capitol Building

Robert de La Salle

1. He came to New France as a young man and fell in love with North America.
2. He wanted to arrive to the Gulf of Mexico from the Mississippi River and claim the land for France.
3. He desired to have the soldiers build forts in the Mississippi Valley to keep the land for France. This settlement grew into the city of New Orleans.
4. He was the first European to make the entire journey down the Mississippi River. The year was 1682.

Father Marquette
by John O'Kane Murray

Nearly three hundred years ago, a little boy, destined to become a great hero, was born in the sunny land of France. Not many days afterwards, he was taken to the parish church to be baptized. His parents, after considerable thought, decided to call him James.

In the course of time, he was sent to school where he proved himself to be a very good student. However, he received most of his religious training from his excellent mother.

At the age of seventeen, he entered the Society of Jesus. After fourteen years spent in studying and teaching, James Marquette had the honor of being raised to the priesthood.

Being endowed with an extraordinary amount of zeal, and having taken the great St. Francis Xavier as his patron and model, he asked his superior to send him to some foreign mission where he might convert the heathens.

His ardent request was granted. Father Marquette landed at Quebec on September 20, 1666. In order to work among the Indians, he spent eighteen months studying the Algonquin and the Huron languages.

Thus equipped he set out for his first mission at Sault Ste. Marie. To get to this place, he had to make a long and painful journey of several hundred miles over rivers, lakes, and wildernesses. There he labored among the Indians for some time.

From other Indians, he learned that his services were badly needed at La Pointe. Here he found the Indians very corrupt and wicked. This, however, did not discourage him. He felt that they needed the refining influence of the religion of Jesus Christ.

Besides endeavoring to convert these Indians, he also tried to collect as much knowledge as he could about the great country to the south of him, and especially about the Mississippi River.

Writing in 1669 to his superior, Father Marquette said: - "When the Illinois come to La Pointe, they pass a large river, almost a league wide. It runs north and south, and so far that the Illinois have never yet heard of its mouth. This great river can hardly empty in Virginia, and we rather believe that its mouth is in California. If the Indians who promised to make me a canoe do not fail to keep their word, we shall go into this river as soon as we can with a Frenchman and a young man, who knows some of the languages; we shall visit the nations which inhabit it, in order to open the way to so many of our Fathers who have long awaited this happiness. This discovery will also give us a complete knowledge of the southern and western sea."

But now Father Marquette's hope of discovering the Mississippi had to be given up for the present. An Indian war broke out, which compelled him to follow the Hurons to Mackinaw where he established the mission of St. Ignatius. Here he waited and prayed for a favorable opportunity to discover the "Father of Waters" and to spread the Gospel among the Indians who lived in its vicinity.

Two years passed away; and one day late in the fall of 1673, a canoe landed at Mackinaw. It contained Louis Joliet, who had orders from the Governor of Canada, to go on the discovery of the Mississippi, taking Father Marquette as his companion and guide.

"The day of the Immaculate Conception of the Holy Virgin," writes the missionary in his journal, "whom I had always invoked since I came to this Ottawa country, to obtain of God the grace to be able to visit the nations on the Mississippi, was the very day on which Mr. Joliet arrived."

The whole winter was spent in making preparations. A rude map of the river was drawn from information received from the Indians, and all facts of any value were carefully made in notebooks.

On the 17th of May, 1673, two canoes, with Father Marquette, Joliet, and five men, set out, and their nimble paddles cut the bright surface of Lake Michigan. They soon reached Green Bay. They proceeded up Fox River, crossed to the Wisconsin, sailed down that stream, and reached the mouth of the long-desired Mississippi, which, says Father Marquette, "we safely entered on the 17th of June, with a joy I cannot express."

As the Jesuit Father and his companions sailed down the Mississippi, they paid particular attention to the strange birds, beasts, fishes, plants, and trees which they saw.

At length, on the 25th of June, they saw footprints on the shore, and a beaten path leading to a beautiful prairie. Here they landed, and leaving their men to take care of the canoes, Father Marquette and Joliet went inland to an Illinois village where they were well received.

Joliet told the Indians that he came from the Governor of Canada, and that Father Marquette was sent to tell them about the Great Spirit. After the usual greetings, the great Sachem arose and said: - "I thank the Black Gown and the Frenchman for taking so much pains to come to visit us; never has the earth been so beautiful, nor the sun so bright as today! I pray you to take pity on me and my nation. You know the Great Spirit Who has made us all. Ask Him to give me life and health, and come and dwell with us that we may know Him."

"This council," says Father Marquette, "was followed by a great feast that consisted of four courses, which we had to take.

"The first course was a great wooden dish of Indian meal boiled in water and seasoned with grease. One of the Indians presented it three or four times to my mouth, as we would do with a little child. He did the same to Mr. Joliet.

"For a second course, he brought in another dish containing three fishes; he took some pains to remove the bones, and having blown upon it to cool it, put it in my mouth, as we would give food to a bird.

"For the third course, they produced a large dog which they had just killed, but learning that we did not eat it, it was withdrawn.

"Finally, the fourth course was a piece of wild

ox, the fattest portions of which were put into our mouths."

Then came the parting. Nearly six hundred Indians went with the priest and his companion to their canoes.

After passing through many adventures and dangers, they reached the mouth of the Arkansas. Here they halted, and resolved to enter. Father Marquette and his companions learned all they wished to know —"that the Mississippi undoubtedly had its mouth in the Gulf of Mexico."

On the 17th of July, the hardy voyagers turned the prows of their canoes about, and began the painful and laborious work of ascending and stemming the currents of the majestic river. Green Bay was reached four months after their departure from it. The distance traveled over was about two thousand six hundred miles.

"Had all the voyage," says Father Marquette, "caused but the salvation of a single soul, I should deem all my fatigue well repaid. This I have reason to think has been done, for, when I was returning, I passed by the Indians of Peoria, who brought me to the water's edge a dying child, which I baptized a little before it expired."

The remaining portion of the story of Father Marquette's heroic life is short, but touching and beautiful. His superhuman labors had broken down his once healthy body. During the winter of 1674, he lay on a sick couch.

When the summer of the same year arrived, and

his health had partly returned, he received the necessary orders to establish a mission among the Illinois.

On the 25th of October, he set out for Kaskaskia. Leaving Green Bay with two men and a number of Indians, he reached the Chicago River in December. Weak in health, with a severe winter staring him in the face, Father Marquette could not think of making the overland journey to Kaskaskia. He determined to winter where .he was, his two faithful French companions remaining with him. A log hut was built - the first human habitation erected on the site of the present great city of Chicago. The priest playfully told them that this was his last voyage, that his end was near.

Hearing of his illness, the Illinois in great grief sent a party of Indians to visit the Black Gown. He received them with extreme kindness, promising to make every effort to reach their village, were it but for a few days.

On the 8th of April, he reached Kaskaskia, and was received as an angel from heaven. On the Monday of Holy Week, he began his instructions. Soon a rustic altar, adorned with pictures of the Blessed Virgin, was erected, and Mass celebrated for the first time in his new mission. Chiefs and warriors, young and old, gathered around their beloved Black Gown; and there, at least, the seeds of the Gospel fell on good ground.

Easter was past, and his Illinois mission established, when the painful sickness returned with renewed force. Well aware that he had reached the boundary line of life, the Jesuit set out for Mackinaw, hoping to die among his fellow missionaries. He passed by the mouth of the St. Joseph River, proceeding to the north along the eastern shore of Lake Michigan. As the two canoemen urged the frail craft over the lonely waters, the sight and strength of the priest gradually failed; "and he was at length so weak that he had to be lifted in and out of his canoe when they landed each night."

"On the eve of his death," writes Father Dablon, "he told them that it would take place on the morrow. During the whole day, he conversed with them about the manner of his burial, the place to be selected for his interment, and how they should raise a cross over his grave.

"They then carried him ashore, kindled a little fire, and raised a poor bark cabin for his use, laying him in it with as little discomfort as they could, but they were so depressed by sadness that, as they afterwards said, they did not know what they were doing.

"The Father being thus stretched on the shore like St. Francis Xavier, as he had always so ardently desired and left alone amid those forests - for his companions were engaged in unloading - he had leisure to repeat all the acts in which he had employed himself during the preceding days.

"When his dear companions afterwards came up, all dejected, he consoled them, and gave them hopes that God would take care of them after his death in those new and unknown countries. He gave them his last instructions, thanked them for all the charity they had shown him during the voyage, begged their pardon in the name of all our Fathers and Brothers in the Ottawa country, and then disposed them to receive the Sacrament of Penance, which he administered to them for the last time.

"He then asked for the holy water and his reliquary, and, taking off his crucifix, which he always wore hanging from his neck, he placed it in the hands of one of his companions, asking him to hold it constantly opposite him , raised before his eyes.

"Feeling that he had but a little while to live, he made a last effort, clasped his hands, and, with his eyes fixed sweetly on his crucifix, he pronounced aloud his profession of faith, and thanked the Divine Majesty for the immense favor He bestowed upon him in allowing him to die in the Society of Jesus, to die in it, as a missionary of Jesus Christ, and above all to die in it, as he had always asked, in a wretched cabin, amid the forests, destitute of all human aid."

His last words were, "Mother of God, remember me."

Thus, on the lone wild shores of Lake Michigan, died, at the age of thirty-eight, on Saturday, the 18th of May, 1675, Father James Marquette, the first explorer of the Mississippi River and the Apostle of the Mississippi Valley.

Father Marquette Looks Down the Mississippi
By Mary Synon

I saw you when the land was young.
  I knew you were a river great;
And so I named you after Her
  Who is the One Immaculate.
I asked the Queen of Heaven to bless
  Your shining path down to the sea,
I asked her aid for men who sought
  To make a new land strong and free.

I watch you now. The land is old.
  Great cities rise beside your stream,
But still I see within your course
  The ancient glory of my dream,
A nation lifting praise to God
  For all His gifts of liberty,
O Mary, Mother of the World ,
  Keep this, your land, forever free!

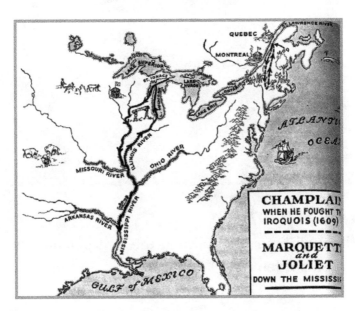

51

The First English Colonies

There were some Englishmen who thought it would be good for England to develop colonies in the New World. A colony is a settlement. When a group of people leave their country, move and settle in a different land, they establish a colony. They are called colonists and remain citizens of the country they came from. The English colonists were subjects of the British ruler.

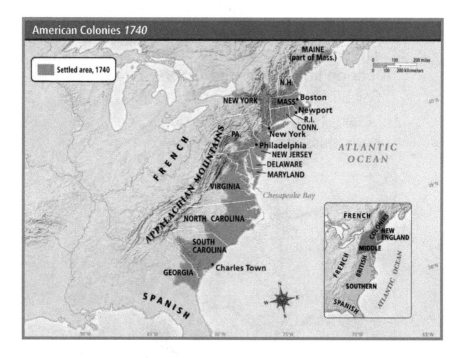

American Colonies 1740

Jamestown (1607)

1. 104 Englishmen established the first permanent English settlement.

2. Many of the men were lazy and started quarrels with the Indians.
3. When winter came they had little food and it looked like they might die of cold and starvation.
4. **John Smith** led the men and he helped the colony become successful.
5. He made the men work and told them: "If you do not work, you shall not eat."
6. They finished the fort that would give them protection from the winter weather.
7. Captain Smith traded beads and tools for food from the Indians so the colonists didn't starve to death.
8. The settlers didn't find the gold they were looking for, but they began to grow tobacco and were able to create a successful tobacco trade with England.
9. In 1619, women arrived to the settlement and many families were formed. Slaves also arrived the same year to be labor for the tobacco and cotton fields.

A Venetian named **John Cabot** sailed across the Atlantic in the name Henry VII in 1497. He claimed land in North America for England.

England also learned more about the New World through **Sir Francis Drake** as he sailed across the world while plundering Spanish ships and settlements.

They Came to Seek Religious Freedom

Jean Leon Gerome Ferris, "The First Thanksgiving"

Because England had a law that everyone who is not worshipping in the Church of England will be punished, many left for the New World to escape persecution for their religion.

Pilgrims: They came on a ship to the New World called the *Mayflower.* They were seeking freedom to practice their religion. They settled in Massachusetts with other Puritans.

Squanto: He was an English-speaking native Indian who taught the Pilgrims how to plant corn and showed them the best places to hunt and fish. He helped the Indians and Pilgrims keep peace among each other. After the Pilgrims' first summer, they shared the first Thanksgiving dinner together with the Indians. They were thankful for God's blessings and the friendship of the Indians.

John Winthrop: a wise leader of the Puritan colony, who planned, directed, and governed the colonies.

Some neighbors moved close to Virginia – the first was **Maryland.**

1. Catholics from England came on two ships in 1634. The ships were called the *Ark* and the *Dove*.

2. The Catholic settlers were happy to find a home where they could freely practice their religion. In England, there were very severe laws against Catholics.

3. These settlers were able to come to North America because an important man lived in England named **Lord Baltimore,** who converted to Catholicism.

4. Lord Baltimore asked the King if he could bring his fellow Catholics to North America to start a colony where they could practice the Faith with freedom. The King granted his request and gave him a large piece of land north of Virginia. The Catholics called it Maryland.

5. This was the first colony to grant freedom of religion. Protestants and Catholics were expected to live in the colony together with peace and respect.

6. The Maryland settlers were able to become friends with the Indians and received much help from them

as they built their homes and started living in the new land.

7. However, some years later the King of England declared that the land no longer belonged to Lord Baltimore, but to England alone and was subject to England's laws. Unfortunately, the Catholics again suffered persecution from the harsh laws against the Faith.

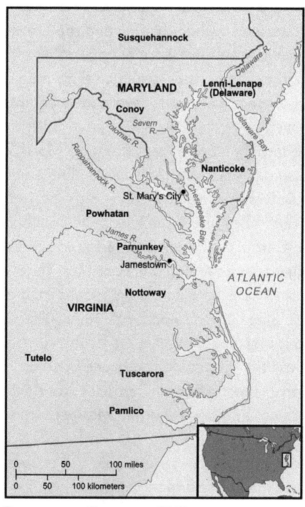

CHESAPEAKE COLONIES, 1640

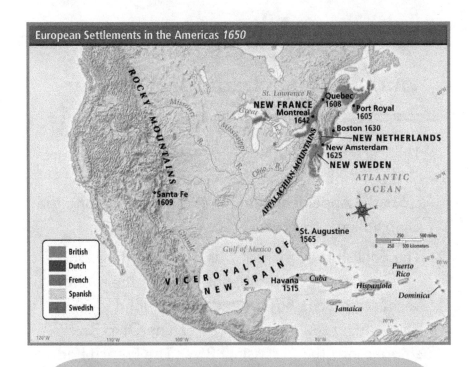

European Settlements in the Americas *1650*

ROCKY MOUNTAINS

St. Lawrence R.
Missouri
Great
NEW FRANCE Quebec 1608
Montreal •Port Royal
1642 1605
Missouri R. •Boston 1630
Ohio R. **NEW NETHERLANDS**
New Amsterdam
1625
NEW SWEDEN
APPALACHIAN MOUNTAINS
ATLANTIC
OCEAN
•Santa Fe
1609
•St. Augustine
1565
Gulf of Mexico
V I C E R O Y A L T Y O F
N E W S P A I N Havana Cuba Puerto
1515 Rico
Hispaniola
Dominica
Jamaica

0 250 500 miles
0 250 500 kilometers

British
Dutch
French
Spanish
Swedish

Spain, France, Holland, and Sweden also had colonies in North America. These people that came to the New World from Europe wanted to remember the countries they were born in. The land that the colonists settled in named their territory from their native country.

There was New France, New Spain, New Amsterdam. People that came from England named their territory New England. In New England, there were different colonies that formed the current states of Massachusetts, Rhode Island, Connecticut, New Hampshire, Maine, and Vermont.

George Washington
and the French and Indian War

1. The thirteen English colonies were along the shores of the Atlantic Ocean. Later, settlers wanted to cross the Appalachian Mountains and live along the Ohio Valley.

2. The English thought this was rightfully their land. However, the French thought this was their land because La Salle had claimed all the land surrounding the Mississippi River. The Ohio River empties into the Mississippi River. The French had forts and soldiers along the Mississippi and Ohio River.

3. In 1753, when George Washington was 21 years

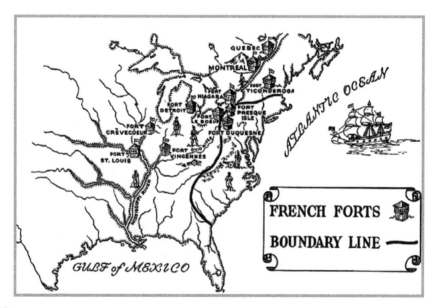

old, the governor of Virginia sent him on an important errand. He wanted George, who was a major in the English army, to deliver a message to the French in the Ohio country. The message would tell the French to stop building forts because the country belonged to England.

4. It was a long and dangerous journey to the Ohio country. He risked his life to deliver the message among harsh weather, rugged terrain, and unfriendly Indians.

5. When the French refused to stop building their forts and claiming the Ohio country as their land, the French and Indian War broke out.

6. The French were outnumbered by the English, but they had many Indians on their side to help them fight. The English had many talented generals to lead their army, and they won the war.

7. The Treaty of Paris of 1763 ended the French and Indian War. A treaty is an agreement between nations for peace.

Maps of the English Colonies

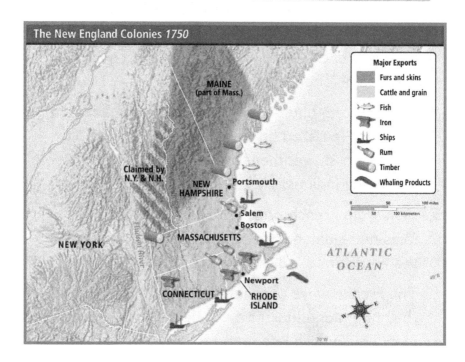

The New England Colonies *1750*

MAINE
(part of Mass.)

Claimed by
N.Y. & N.H.

NEW YORK

NEW
HAMPSHIRE

Portsmouth

Salem
Boston

MASSACHUSETTS

CONNECTICUT

Newport

RHODE
ISLAND

ATLANTIC
OCEAN

Major Exports

Furs and skins
Cattle and grain
Fish
Iron
Ships
Rum
Timber
Whaling Products

A Reason for the French and Indian War

The English took over the Dutch lands around the Hudson and Mohawk Rivers and got rich in the fur trade. Soon the animals became fewer in the New York area.

The best lands for furs were around the Great Lakes and Ohio River. The French owned this land, not the English. The English became jealous and became one of their reasons to enter a war over land with the French. Animals good for furs were beaver, bobcat, mink, muskrat, and otter.

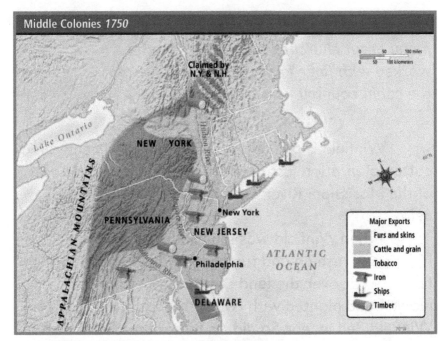

Middle Colonies *1750*

Claimed by N.Y. & N.H.

Lake Ontario

NEW YORK

APPALACHIAN MOUNTAINS

PENNSYLVANIA

NEW JERSEY

New York

Philadelphia

ATLANTIC OCEAN

DELAWARE

Major Exports
- Furs and skins
- Cattle and grain
- Tobacco
- Iron
- Ships
- Timber

Trouble began between the government in England and the colonists when the English parliament started making laws on taxes to help pay for the expense of the French and Indian War. The Stamp Act was passed in 1765.

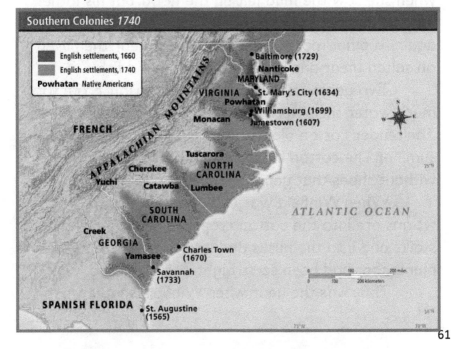

Southern Colonies *1740*

- English settlements, 1660
- English settlements, 1740
- **Powhatan** Native Americans

Baltimore (1729)

Nanticoke

MARYLAND

APPALACHIAN MOUNTAINS

VIRGINIA St. Mary's City (1634)

Powhatan

Williamsburg (1699)

Monacan Jamestown (1607)

FRENCH

Tuscarora

Cherokee NORTH CAROLINA

Yuchi

Catawba Lumbee

SOUTH CAROLINA

ATLANTIC OCEAN

Creek

GEORGIA

Yamasee Charles Town (1670)

Savannah (1733)

SPANISH FLORIDA St. Augustine (1565)

Our American people have built
many great churches, but none of them
worked with finer faith than the people of
the cabin country who built the

Church in the Cotton Fields

Winfield is ten years old. He lives in a cabin on a cotton plantation just north of the land at the mouth of the Mississippi River. That land is called the river delta.

When Winfield was four years old the Mississippi, rushing and tumbling and leaping in spring flood, swept over the land that his father had just plowed and planted with cotton seed.
Winfield fled in fear. So did his father and mother and his sisters, Rose and Annie, and his brother Terry. When the waters of the river slipped back within their banks, his family came back to the cabin. His mother cried when she saw the mud left by the flood, but his father hitched the mule before the old plow and started out again to plant more cotton seed. That year they lived on salted meat and coffee and bread and fish.

Two years later came the dry season. From too much water they were cut down to no water at all. The tender cotton plants dried out in that long, hot summer. The cotton blossoms died. The children went without shoes that year.

When Winfield was eight years old, little white worms ate into the cotton crop. They dug into the stalks and into the husks and into the seeds of the plants that had been so straight and so strong.

That was the year when Winfield's father lost

the little plantation. He had borrowed money from the store to pay for tools and for seed and for food. When the crop failed, the store asked him for money. He had none. With his shoulders stooped from worry and his head bent low with trouble, Winfield's father hitched the mule to the old cart and drove to a town ten miles away. He sold the farm to pay his debts. They stayed on in the shabby little cabin. Winfield's father received tools and seeds and supplies from the new owner of the land in exchange for his work. He had little pay. That year again they lived on salted meat and bread and fish. They had no coffee.

That was the year when Father John came to the river delta. Winfield will never forget the morning when he first saw Father John.

It was almost the end of the season, and the boy was picking cotton in the field near the river road, dragging his sack after him, when an old black car drew up at the fence rail. Winfield pulled off his wide-brimmed straw hat and stared silently at the man who was getting out of the car to speak to him.

Father John leaned against the fence rail and questioned the bashful boy. He asked him about his father and his mother, and about all the boys and girls who lived along the river. He wanted to know if any of them had been baptized. He asked if they had enough to eat and enough to wear.

Winfield stood first on one bare foot and then on the other, but he answered the young priest. He heard Father John sigh. He saw the sorrow in Father John's eyes as he told the stories of the cabins along the river. Even before Father John rode away with a promise to return, Winfield knew that he had found a friend.

There was no Catholic church in the community. There never had been one along that stretch of river road. "We will build one," Father John had told the boy. "We will build a church and a school. They will belong to all the people."

So, helped by the priest's holiness and friendly kindness, the people of the delta built the church.

Winfield's father led the other men to the best lumber in the swamps, and there they cut down the trees. They hauled them to a sawmill, where the trunks were cut into boards. They carried them back again, up the road past Winfield's cabin, to the high ground chosen by Father John for the church.

They never stopped to think, as they labored for the young priest, that not one of them was a Catholic. But Father John knew, as he labored beside them, that he was working for their souls.

"Some day you will all be Catholics here," he told Winfield. "Saint Isidore will help me to lead the way." Then he told the boy about Saint Isidore the Plowman. The boy, his eyes wide with wonder, listened to the story of the farmer who had lived many hundred years ago.

Winfield told his brother Terry about Saint Isidore and his feast day. He told Rose and Annie. He told his mother. He told his father.

"Saint Isidore lived a long time ago in the far country of Spain," Winfield told them. "He was a poor farmer like our own father, and he worked in the fields. He was so good that all the great people of the city looked up to him.

"He helped everyone. He took care of the poor and the sick. He was kind to orphan children, and he shared with them the little he had. He taught them how to plant and plow and reap.

"He did so much work that people said that angels helped him when he plowed. He was a poor farmer, but when he died, the people of Spain were sad. For days and nights thousands of men and women and children came to see him for the last time. They said, 'Isidore was a saint.' The Catholic church called him a saint, and so he has been Saint Isidore to all the whole wide world."

"When is the feast day of Saint Isidore?" asked Winfield's father.

"Father John says that it comes in March," Winfield told him. His father made a promise. "The church will be finished on that day," he said.

Everybody worked. Winfield's father and the other men from the river plantations sang as they hammered and sawed wood and drove in nails to build the church. Winfield's mother and all the other women from the cabins painted and varnished the floors and the benches. Winfield and his brother Terry and even Rose and Annie carried great pails of water.

They worked by day and by night. On the evening before the feast day of the saint of Spain, the golden cross was set in place on the steeple of the church in the cabin country. The church was finished.

Winfield told again the story of Saint Isidore.

Before the sun was in the sky on Sunday morning, Winfield was on his way to the first Mass in the new church. Beside him walked his father and mother and Rose and Annie and Terry. After him, on horseback. , on muleback, in wagons, and in old cars, came their neighbors and friends.

They heard the new bell.

They entered the church they had built, the church which was their own.

They stood silently, or knelt clumsily, as Father John read the service of the Sacrifice of the Mass.

Then in the gold and white of his vestments, he turned to speak to them. He thanked them for their help. He told them of his desire to serve them. His voice was deep and low as he went on. He knew their problems, he said. He had been a boy on a farm, and so he could speak of crops and failures. Then he told them of the joys of farm life, the look of the wide sky, the songs of the birds, the friendliness of animals, the kindness of neighbors.

He held out to them, as their eyes turned toward the little pulpit, a hope of escape from the long discouragements. He told them of ways to control the little white worms and to fight failure and waste.

He told them of the school he would build for the children, and he told them of his hopes and his dreams.

Then with tears in his eyes, he told them about Faith and about God. He told them of God's love for them, of their place as brothers under God the Father.

Men would one day understand that, and everyone would be better and happier.

He began to pray.

Their voices, not yet familiar with the words, were slow to repeat them. "Our Father, Who art in Heaven, hallowed be Thy Name," he said.

"Our Father, Who art in Heaven," they answered him.

As he finished the age-old prayer he stood on the steps that led toward the rough stone altar and blessed them. "May God bless you," he said.

A light, brighter than sunrise over the Mississippi, shone in the eyes of Winfield, and of his father and his mother, and of Rose and Annie, and of his brother Terry.

"Amen," they said.

John Singer Sargent, "Carnation Lily Lily Rose"

War for Independence
The American Revolution

Emanuel Leutze, "Washington Crossing the Delaware"

1. The colonists didn't like the idea of the government in England making the laws when the government was so far away. Their life was very different from life in England. The colonists wanted to make their own laws. The colonists began protesting the taxes.

2. In the fall of 1774, the colonists met in **Philadelphia**. Men from almost every colony came. This important meeting was called the First **Continental Congress**. They made a list of complaints and sent it to the government in England. They also agreed they all would stop trading their goods with England.

3. The colonies began to unite together. It was important for them to stand together in their fight with England. They began preparing for battle with supplies and training. The first battles of the war were fought in **Concord** and **Lexington.**

4. In the spring of **1775**, the colonists met in Philadelphia again. This meeting was called the **Second Continental Congress.** This time, they agreed that they could not expect just laws from their king in England and Parliament. They decided that they must break away from their mother country and fight for freedom as their own nation.

Independence Hall, Philadelphia

5. The members of Congress also chose George Washington to be the Commander-in-Chief of the American army. He had to sacrifice his pleasant life at Mount Vernon to lead the soldiers. He would be cold, hungry, tired, and often risking his life. He chose to make this sacrifice for independence and good of his fellow colonists.

6. George was given a hard task, but God had given him many talents and he was a hard worker. He was a good planner and very brave. He cheered his

Congress asked **Thomas Jefferson** to write the Declaration of Independence. In the Declaration, he wrote: *"We hold these truths to be self-evident, that all men are created equal, that they are endowed by their Creator with certain unalienable Rights, that among these are Life, Liberty and the pursuit of Happiness."*

On July 4, 1776, the members of Congress voted to adopt it and this is now celebrated as the birthday of the United States of America.

Thomas Jefferson became the third President of the United States.

The Delaware River was
filled with danger
on the Christmas night when
Young Patrick tried to find

A Boat for the General
The Boy at the Ferry

On that Christmas morning Young Patrick served Father Farmer's .Mass at the settlement near the ferry on the Delaware River.

There were only a few people at Mass, old men, and the women and children. All the younger men were soldiers in General Washington's army in camp near Philadelphia.

Times were bad for the Americans. The British soldiers were camped across the Delaware. General Washington had moved his soldiers into Pennsylvania, but Philadelphia was in danger. The British, in great numbers, would cross the Delaware on the ice as soon as the river froze. They would win the war, and freedom would be lost.

Patrick knew this well because his grandfather, Old Patrick, often talked of what might happen. Old Patrick was the man who ran the ferry across the river. He knew many of the soldiers. He even knew General Washington. "God bless and save him," he always said when he spoke of him. "May the good Lord help him to win our freedom!"

Young Patrick thought of his grandfather's words as he came out from the little store where Mass had been said. The river was not yet frozen, but it was thick with ice. If the cold grew greater and the ice became solid , the British would be able to cross on it. Then what would become of the people of all the Thirteen Colonies?

Father Farmer had already gone back to Philadelphia, but a few old men and some of the women stood outside the store. One of the men asked Patrick, "Where is your grandfather?"

"I do not know," the boy said. "A messenger came for him in the night."

"Then you are alone?" one of the women asked. "Will you not come home with us and share the dinner we have? This is Christmas, and a boy should not be alone."

"Thank you," Patrick said, "but my grandfather will be coming home, and he may need me."

There was little food in the house, he knew, and he was not sure when Old Patrick would return. But he knew that something important might soon happen, and, if it did, his grandfather might need him.

"Keep close," Old Patrick had told him the day before. "I do not know when I may need a boy for a man's errand."

"I can do any errand you give me, Grandfather," Young Patrick said.

"We'll see," said Old Patrick.

Through the afternoon the boy waited alone in the quiet house. The cold grew greater, and he sometimes opened the door to see if the river were frozen. It was not yet solid, but great cakes of ice were piling up in it.

"The British will soon be coming," Young Patrick thought.

It was almost dark when his grandfather came home. The boy started to heat some soup in the kettle over the fire, but the old man stopped him.

"I have no time for food," he said. "Tonight is the night, lad."

"For what?" the boy asked.

"Can you keep a secret?" Old Patrick asked, then gave his own answer. "You have always done what I told you. You will do it now." He rubbed his hands and stamped his feet to make himself warmer. "General Washington will cross the river," he said.

"Tonight?" the boy cried.

"Tonight. He is going to surprise the British soldiers. This is his only chance. If he can win the battle tonight, we may save Philadelphia and our freedom. If he does not-"

"He will win," said Young Patrick. "Are you going to take him over the river?"

"No," the old man said. "Last night I took him in my ferry so that he could see the best place for landing the troops on the other side. Tonight he will cross the river with his soldiers. I have been gathering the boats for them. There are still many to find. You can help me, lad."

"For the general?" Young Patrick cried. "For General Washington?"

"For him or his men," Old Patrick answered. He found a piece of paper and began to mark it with a coal. "We have hidden many boats here," he said, pointing to a spot on the map he drew. "Friends will bring some rafts from Philadelphia, but we need more boats if we are to carry all of the General's men. I can get some. You will help me find more."

"A boat?" the boy cried. "A boat that General Washington can use for himself? I know where there is a boat like that. It is a fine, grand boat."

The old man looked surprised . "Where is it?"

"Down the river. I know the place," answered the boy eagerly.

"Who owns it?" asked his grandfather.

"Robert Wilson," the boy replied.

"The boat belongs to Robert's uncle," said Old Patrick.

"No, sir," said Young Patrick. "The boat is Robert's. It was his father's boat. His father left it to him."

"His uncle uses it, and his uncle is for the British," said the grandfather.

"But Robert owns the boat, and he is not for the British. He has told me so," said Young Patrick.

"It is a big boat, lad, bigger than you can handle," sighed the old man.

"Robert will help me. Where shall we bring it, sir?" asked the boy.

"If you can get it, and handle it, bring it to the old ferry landing. You'll have to work fast. We must cross the river before the British can find out what we plan . Be careful, lad," warned Old Patrick.

"I shall, sir," promised the boy.

"God speed you," the old man said.

Patrick's Errand

Snow was falling as Young Patrick ran down the road beside the river. As he went, he looked sharply and saw some of the boats Old Patrick had found. There were not many of them, the boy saw, and he wondered if General Washington would be able to win a battle with the few men he could take across the river.

He would need every boat they could find, and for himself the general would need the strongest boat of all. That meant the boat Robert Wilson owned. It was the best boat on the river.

Robert, like Young Patrick, was an orphan. He lived with his uncle, but the house and everything in it was Robert's. The boy was older, bigger, and stronger than Young Patrick. With him the boy would be able to take the boat to the old ferry landing. There it would wait for General Washington.

The snow beat harder against the boy as he left the village. The houses were few, and darkness was coming. He tried to run, but his boots were wet and heavy. Sometimes he saw men coming on the road, and he hid until they had passed. He dared not meet them if they were friendly to the British.

Darkness was all around him when he came to the Wilson house. There was one light there, in the room he knew to be the kitchen. He moved toward it carefully.

Then he whistled the call he used for Robert. In a moment the kitchen door opened and Robert stood in the light.

"Are you alone?" Patrick asked him in a low voice.

"No one is with me," said Robert. "My uncle has gone to Philadelphia." He seemed to find it hard to move. "Come in," he told Patrick.

"May we use your boat tonight?" Patrick asked him.

"My boat? Tonight? For what?" Robert questioned.

"You want freedom, do you not?"

"I do," said Robert. "But what has my boat to do with it?"

"You will tell no one? Promise!"

"I promise. But why?" asked Robert again.

"General Washington will take his troops across the river tonight. He will fight the British in Trenton. He needs every boat he can get. He needs yours," begged Patrick.

"He can have it." Robert Wilson's face grew bright. "But how can you get it to him?"

"You and I can take it to the old ferry landing. He will come there," explained Young Patrick.

"You will have to take it alone, Patrick," Robert Wilson said.

"You will not help me?" asked Patrick sadly.

"I cannot. I fell yesterday and hurt ·my back so badly I can hardly move. That is why I did not go to Philadelphia. You may use the boat, but I cannot go with you," replied Robert.

For a moment Young Patrick stood silent. How could he take out this big boat and steer it through the ice of the river? With Robert's help it could be done. But how could a boy, alone, get the boat out into the water?

"You mean you cannot help me?" he asked Robert.

"I wish I could," the older boy said. "I cannot even walk to the shore with you."

Sadly Young Patrick walked to the shore where the boat rested. It was a big boat, and it looked twice its size now. How could he push it down into the icy water? And how could he row it through the ice of the river?

"God help me," he prayed. "Show me a way to do what I must do."

Danger on the River

The boat seemed frozen on the sand. Patrick dared not build a fire near it. He had to push and pull, push and pull. The snow came down heavier. Every push, every pull grew harder. Would he ever be able to move the boat?

At last it gave way a little, then a little more. He worked harder and harder. The boat moved nearer the water. Then, with his body aching with pain, Young Patrick gathered all his strength and pushed the heavy boat into the river.

He found his way to the oars and took one in each hand. He had never known before how big they were. They were so heavy that he could hardly move them. His arms ached, his shoulders ached, his back ached, but he kept on trying. The boat moved a little out from the shore.

All around it floated the cakes of ice. Some of them which had not looked large from the shore looked huge from the boat. How would he be able to get around them when he had no one to steer?

Little by little, the boat moved. It was a. good boat. Young Patrick had been right in saying it was one of the best on the river. But it was a heavy boat, and the boy sometimes felt that he was not moving it.

Every little while a great cake of ice bumped against

the boat and almost wrecked it. Young Patrick could swim, but he knew he would not be able to swim in the icy water. If the boat turned over, he was lost.

His hands grew so cold that he could hardly move the oars. He told himself that he must be brave. Sometimes he thought he did not move the boat at all. Other times he thought that he moved it a little.

Once in a while he heard sounds on the shore, but he dared not cry out. If any friend of the British heard him, his errand would fail. He could not cry for help. He must go on as long as he could.

One of the oars slipped from his hand, but he caught it in time. If it had been lost, he would have no chance to move the boat. General Washington needed this boat for the crossing of the river.

"God help me," Young Patrick kept praying. "God help our country! Help us to win our freedom! Help us this Christmas night!

Sleet and snow fell around him, on the boat, on the river ice, and most of all, on his wet clothing. It froze on his cheeks and his hands. His teeth chattered with the cold. The oars grew so heavy that he could hardly lift them.

He grew sleepy, but he knew he must not close his eyes. "If I sleep, I die," he thought. But his head drooped, and his eyes closed. Then an oar slipped from his hand.

He did not hear the sound of other oars in the water. He did not see the men who leaped from another boat and set back the oar that had slipped. He did not know that they brought him in to the shore at the old ferry landing.

His grandfather was standing near him when he awoke. "You brought it, lad," Old Patrick said. "But how did you bring it alone on such a night?

A tall man in uniform stood beside Old Patrick. "You are a brave boy," the tall man said. "Thank you, my lad."

"Ready, General?" asked Old Patrick.

The tall man moved toward the boat. Other men joined him and crowded into it. Two men took the oars, and the boat moved into the water, out among the great, white cakes of ice.

General Washington stood in the boat as it drew away. He was looking across the river, thinking, perhaps, of the battle he must give the British. Once, and only once, he turned back. He waved to Old Patrick ' and Young Patrick.

"God save him," Old Patrick said.

"God save him," said Young Patrick.

He was no longer tired and cold. He had forgotten the ache in his arms, in his shoulders, in his back. All he remembered was that he had helped the general when the general had needed that help.

"I'm in General Washington's army," he told his grandfather.

"I think," Old Patrick said, "that you are in his navy."

They watched the boat go toward Trenton and the victory that would help to win freedom for the land they loved.

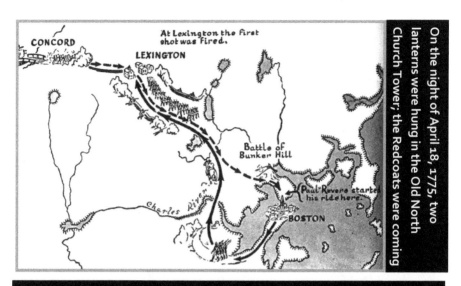

At Lexington the first shot was fired.

CONCORD

LEXINGTON

Battle of Bunker Hill

Paul Revere started his ride here.

Charles River

BOSTON

The British wanted their three armies to invade New York at Albany. The first was to come down from Canada; the second was to go up from New York City; the third was to come across the Mohawk Valley from Lake Ontario. They wanted to cut off New England from the other states.

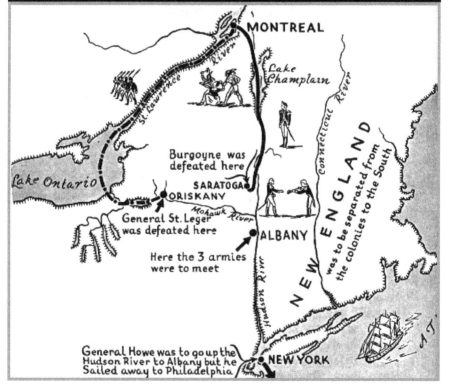

MONTREAL

Lake Champlain

St. Lawrence River

Connecticut River

Burgoyne was defeated here

SARATOGA

ORISKANY

Lake Ontario

General St. Leger was defeated here

Mohawk River

ALBANY

Here the 3 armies were to meet

N E W   E N G L A N D

was to be separated from the colonies to the South

Hudson River

General Howe was to go up the Hudson River to Albany but he Sailed away to Philadelphia

NEW YORK

80

In October 1781, British general—General Cornwallis—surrendered his entire army to Washington in Yorktown, Virginia.

The Treaty of Paris in 1783 between Americans and British, which gave the U.S. all the lands between the Atlantic Ocean and the Mississippi .

The Beginnings of a New Nation

1. In the spring of 1787, the new independent United States of America held a very important meeting. Congress had men represent the citizens from each of the 13 states. They wanted to unite the states and form one country.

2. This meeting is called the **Constitutional Convention** because the men wrote our country's Constitution. A constitution contains the basic laws or rules of a country.

3. George Washington was elected the President of the Convention.

4. In 1788, the **United States Constitution** was adopted as the law of the land. It was declared that the new nation should have a Congress, a Supreme Court, and a President. These are the three branches of our government: executive, legislative, and judicial. George Washington received every vote during the election of the First President.

5. During Washington's presidency, a beautiful piece of land by the Potomac River was chosen as the place for the new country's capital city. This is called the **District of Colombia,** or Washington D.C, named after our great first president.

"Scene at the Signing of the Constitution of the United States"

Like Washington

We cannot all be Washingtons,
    And have our birthdays celebrated;
But we can love the things he loved,
    And we can hate the things he hated.

He told the truth, he hated lies,
    He minded what his mother taught him,
And every day he tried to do
    The simple duties that it brought him.

Perhaps the reason little folks
    Are sometimes great when they grow taller,
Is just because, like Washington,
    They do their best when they are smaller.

The Carrolls

1. **Charles Carroll:** His grandfather settled in Maryland. He was Catholic and had other Catholic cousins, Daniel and John. They were taught by the Jesuit priests. God gave him a very good intellect. He had a great ability to write and speak to help others learn about good principles. He attended the Continental Congress and signed the Declaration of Independence. He had the idea of placing the capital of the United States near the Potomac River.

2. **Daniel Carroll:** He served as a representative of Maryland at the Constitutional Convention. He played an important role in the Convention. He argued that there should be three branches of government and that the President ought to be elected by the American people, not Congress. He gave his own land to the United States to build the capitol. Some of the government buildings in Washington D.C. were built on what used to be his farmland.

Bishop Carroll lays the cornerstone for the Cathedral of the Assumption in Baltimore

3. **Bishop John Carroll:** He was Daniel's younger brother. While studying in school, he

felt God was calling him to be a priest. When he served as a priest in Maryland, Catholics were very restricted in the practice of their Faith. He would travel the countryside to bring the Sacraments to the Catholics since they weren't allowed to have a church. John became a good friend of Benjamin Franklin while traveling together to Canada. Fr. John was chosen by the Pope to be the first bishop of the United States; he became the Bishop of Baltimore, Maryland. The other dioceses of the new United States were Boston, New York, Philadelphia, and Bardstown.

Gilbert Munger, The Great Falls of the Potomac River

Mother Elizabeth Ann Seton

Elizabeth Ann Bayley was born in New York in 1774. She was baptized in the Protestant Episcopal Church . Her father was a doctor, and sadly, her mother died when she was only three years old. She became one of the first American citizens when the country announced the Declaration of Independence on July 4, 1776.

Elizabeth's father helped take care of the wounded soldiers during the American War for Independence. Her father always helped poor families and taught his young daughter to be kind and charitable to those who needed help.

When Elizabeth grew to be a very good and beautiful young woman, she fell in love with William Seton. They got married in 1794 when she was 19 years old. A year later, they had their first child—Anna Maria. They soon grew to be a very happy and large family of seven. Elizabeth was also a close friend of William's sister, Rebecca Seton. Together, they helped the poor in New York City and formed a society to help poor widows with small children.

After some happy years together, William's ship

business was not doing well and he became seriously ill. Desperate for his recovery, she took a trip to Italy with him, hoping the mild climate would help him. He died soon after they arrived.

However, even in this dark time of Elizabeth's life, God was watching over her and her family. She found help from a family in Italy. They were Catholics and shared with her the beautiful truths of the Faith, most importantly, the Real Presence of Jesus in the Holy Eucharist and the Blessed Mother. Elizabeth would go to Mass with her new friends and witnessed the glories of Catholic worship and gave her a deep peace and joy.

When she returned to New York, she continued to seek the truth and entered the Catholic Church in 1805. When she became Catholic, many of her Protestant friends and relatives abandoned her and would not help her with her 5 children. She began to teach at a school, and later opened a boarding house, despite the anger of many Protestant people.

She was a good teacher and Bishop John Carroll invited her to begin a teaching order for girls. She opened the first free school in America. After she pronounced her vows of poverty, chastity, and obedience she was then called by all "Mother Seton." Her and her sisters continued to help teach and take care of young girls in the United States, establishing orphanages and schools. She is the first native-born American to be declared a saint.

Keep Up Your Courage
By Alice Dalgliesh

Sarah lay on a quilt under a tree. The darkness was all around her, but through the branches she could see one bright star. It was comfortable to look at.

The spring night was cold, and Sarah drew her warm cloak close. That was comfortable, too. She thought of how her mother had put it around her the day she and her father started out on this long, hard journey.

"Keep up your courage," her mother had said, fastening the cloak under Sarah's chin. "Keep up your courage, Sarah Noble!"

And, indeed, Sarah needed to keep up her courage, for she and her father were going all the way into the wilderness of Connecticut to build a house.

Finally they had come to the last day of the journey. The Indian trail had been narrow; the hills went up and down, up and down. Sarah and her father were tired, and even Thomas, the brown horse, walked wearily.

By late afternoon they would be home. Home? No, it wasn't really home, just a place out in the wilderness. But 'after a while it would be home; John Noble told Sarah it would be. His voice kept leading her on.

"Now we must be about two miles away."

"Now it is surely a mile ... only a mile."

Sarah's tired feet seemed to dance. She picked some wild flowers and stuck them in the harness behind Thomas's ear.

"You must be well dressed, Thomas," she said. "We are coming home."

She put a pink flower on her own dress and her feet danced along again. Then suddenly she stopped.

"Father, if there is no house, where shall we live?" Her father smiled down at her. "I have told you ...."

"Then tell me again. I like to hear."

"I hope to find a cave in the side of a hill," he said. "I will make a hut for us, and a fence around it. Then you and Thomas and I will live there until the house is built. Though Thomas will have to help me with the building."

Sarah laughed. "Thomas cannot build a house!" She had a funny picture in her mind of solemn, long-faced Thomas carefully putting the logs in place.

"He can drag logs," her father said. "Soon we shall have a fine house."

Now they had come to the top of a long, steep hill and they stopped at a place where there were not many trees, only bushes and coarse grass.

"This is one of the bare places," John Noble said. "The Indians have cleared it for a hunting ground."

Sarah looked around her fearfully. Behind the bushes something stirred. . . .

"A deer," said her father, and raised his gun. But Sarah clung to him.

"No, Father, no! Do not shoot it!" "But we must have meat...."

"Not now, not now," Sarah begged. "Its eyes are so gentle, Father."

"Well ..." said John Noble. But he did not shoot

The deer rushed away, its white tail showing like a flag. Then Sarah drew a long breath and looked down.

Below there was a valley. "And you would see the Great River if it were not for the trees," her father said.

Sarah looked and looked and filled her mind with the beauty of it. It was a beauty that would stay with her all her life. Beyond the valley there were green hills, and beyond ... and beyond ... and beyond ... more hills of a strange, soft, and misty blue.

The trees were the dark green of firs and the light green of birches in springtime. And now they were friendly. They were not like the angry dark trees that had seemed to stand in their path as they came.

"I do like it," Sarah said. "And I do not see any Indians."

"The Indians are by the Great River," her father said. "And I have told you, Sarah, they are good Indians."

John Noble took Sarah's small, cold hand in his.

"There are people in this world who do not help others along the way, Sarah, while there are those who do. In our home all will be treated with kindness always, Sarah. The Indians, too, and they will not harm us."

Now Sarah held her courage a little more firmly. She also held tightly to her father's hand. And so they came, with Thomas, down the long hill into the place that would be their home.

It was a fair piece of land with the trees already cleared. Men had come over from Milford, on the coast, to buy the land from the Indians. They had cleared it and divided it into plots for the houses. The land sloped down to the Great River, and beyond the river were the Indian fields.

It was in the hill across the river that Sarah and her father found a place hollowed out, that would do for the night.

"And tomorrow I will make it larger and build a shed and a fence," John Noble said. They took from Thomas the heavy load he had been carrying-bedding and pots, seeds for planting, tools, and warm clothes for the weather that would be coming.

For some days John Noble was busy making the cave a good place to live. He built a shed with a strong fence around it. He made, too, rough beds of logs, and a table and stools. Sarah took delight in it all.

But after it was done, he said to her, "I must begin the work on the house. It should be finished before winter. You will not mind staying here, Sarah, while Thomas and I work?"

Sarah did mind, but she did not say so. There was still the question of Indians. On the hill and along the river they could see the bark-covered houses. People moved about among the houses, but no Indians had come near the cave. She knew, though, that her father had spoken with some of the men.

She did not want her father to go, but the house must be built. So she looked at him steadily and said, "I will stay here, Father." But to herself she was saying, "Keep up your courage, Sarah Noble. Keep up your courage! "

Then John Noble and Thomas went across the river at a place where it was not deep. They went on up the hill, and Sarah was alone. For a little while she did not know what to do. Then she took out the Bible they had brought with them. It was a book full of wonderful stories. Which should she read? She liked the story of Sarah, whose namesake she was. Sarah had a son named Isaac. That was a scary story, but it came out all right in the end.

Then there was the story of David and how he killed the giant .... Oh, it was hard to choose.

Sarah sat on a stool at the entrance to the shed, the Bible on her lap. So she had often sat and read to her doll, Arabella, and to her little sister, who never would listen. Here there was not anyone to listen-not anyone, not even Arabella, for there had been no room to bring her.

The early June air was mild, but Sarah felt suddenly that she needed her cloak. So she got it, and sat down again.

No one to listen-but she would read to herself. She opened the Bible and there was one of the stories she loved best of all.

It was the story of the boy Samuel and of how the Lord called to him in the night. Sarah thought of the Lord as a kind old man like her grandfather. Her mother said no one knew how He looked, but Sarah was sure she knew. She wished He would speak to her as He had to Samuel. That would be exciting. What in the world would she answer?

Sarah read on and on. And then the sounds began. There was a rustling and a sound of feet coming quietly nearer and nearer. . . .

Sarah held tightly to the book and pulled her cloak

around her. Rustle-rustle .... Suddenly Sarah saw a bright eye peering at her through a chink in the log fence.

INDIANS! They were all around her; some of them crowded in the opening of the palisade. But they were young Indians, not any older than she was. Still, there were many of them. . . . Sarah kept as still as a rabbit in danger. The children came in, creeping nearer, creeping nearer, like small brown field mice, until they were all around Sarah, looking at her. Sarah closed the book and sat very still. Then she remembered what her father had said as they stood on the hill.

"Good morning," she said politely, "you are welcome to our house."

The Indian children stared at her. Then they came nearer. Soon Sarah found that all around her was a ring of children, standing and sitting, staring, staring with their dark eyes.

The children stared; Sarah began to feel as if their eyes were going all the way through her.

Keep up your courage, Sarah Noble. She thought the words to herself. Here she was in the wilderness with all these Indians around her. She wished the Lord would speak to her as He had to young Samuel. He would tell her what to do.

The Lord did not speak out loud, or at least Sarah did not hear Him. But all at once she knew what to do. She opened the book and began to read to the children. They came nearer and nearer.

They like the story, Sarah thought. They will not hurt me because they like the story. She read and read, and the children listened, because the sound of her voice was strange and pleasant.

Then the story was over and Sarah closed the Bible. Still the children sat and stared and said not a word.

"My name," said Sarah clearly, "is Sarah Noble."

One of the boys said something; then another spoke. Sarah did not understand a word of their strange talk.

"How foolish," she said aloud, "why can't you speak English?"

Perhaps some of her impatience crept into her voice, for the spell was broken. Like the deer when her father lifted the gun, the children were off and away.

Sarah sat there by herself and now she really felt alone.

"Oh," she said to herself. "I wish they would come again!" And she shook her head. "For shame, Sarah Noble, I fear you were not polite. Perhaps they will never come back."

The Indian children did come, again and again. Sarah soon lost all fear of them, and they of her.

Old Log House
By James S. Tippett

On a little green knoll
At the edge of the wood
My great-great-grandmother's
First house stood.

The house was of logs
My grandmother said
With one big room
And a lean-to shed.

The logs were cut
And the house was raised
By pioneer men
In the olden days.

They split the shingles;
They filled each chink;
It's a house of which
I like to think.

Forever and ever
I wish I could
Live in a house
At the edge of a wood.

Thomas Cole, Home in the Woods

95

Fr. Juniperro Serra: he belonged to the religious order called Franciscans. He is one of the most famous Spanish priests in the New World.

In 1769, he arrived at the harbor of San Diego, California. He built nine missions during his life as a missionary. The missions were connected by a narrow footpath called *El Camino Real*.

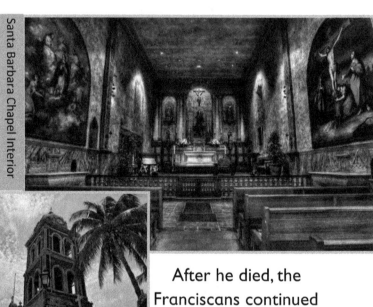

Santa Barbara Chapel Interior

After he died, the Franciscans continued building missions throughout California. They completed 21 missions total.

During Fr. Serra's life, the United States of America was just winning its independence. Father Serra didn't know very much about the United States. California and the United States were separated by many miles of land with forests, plains, rivers, deserts, mountains.

As the United States grew, Americans moved farther west and came closer and closer to California. When the first settlers arrived in southern California, they found some of the Franciscan missions still standing and were welcomed by the missionaries. At this time, California was still a part of Mexico.

In 1848, this land became a part of the United States at the end of the Mexican War.

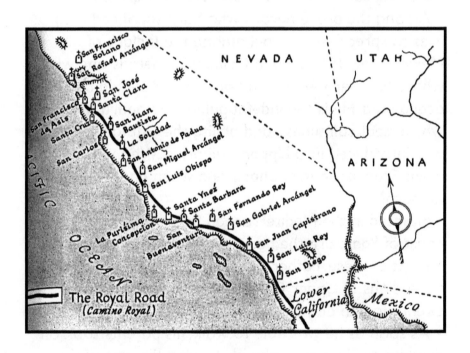

Father Juniperro Serra

Among the first Catholic missionaries to come to America with the Spaniards, we find the intrepid sons of St. Francis. The work which these zealous priests accomplished in the early years of the settlement of this continent has received but scant notice in the pages of history. How they labored among the half-savage Indians, how they taught them to read and to write, as well as to cultivate the land; how they won them from their pagan and idolatrous practices, is generally summed up in a few brief paragraphs.

Among the brave heroes who have sacrificed their lives to spread the Gospel among the Indians of Mexico, New Mexico, and California, there is one with whose life every American boy and girl should be acquainted. He is the indefatigable missionary through whose zeal, saintliness, and ability the Catholic religion was introduced into Upper California. Who was this great Franciscan missionary, and when and where was he born?

Situated in the Mediterranean Sea off the eastern coast of Spain are the beautiful Balearic Islands. In the largest of these, Father Juniperro Serra, the Apostle of the Indians of Upper California, was born on the twenty-fourth day of November in the year 1713.

As soon as he was able to walk, his parents took on Sundays to the parish church. During the rest of the week, the little boy kept them busy answering his many questions about the different pictures he saw in the church. His father and mother were delighted to speak about these holy subjects. They felt from the beginning that their son might one day become priest.

A few years later, what a source of pleasure it must have been to his parents to see him assist the priest at Mass as an altar boy! At an early age, he made up his mind that he would become a Franciscan, if it were God's holy will.

At school in Palma, the future Franciscan made giant stride: in his studies. In a short time, his wonderful progress made him the pride of his teachers. But even though he was deeply engrossed in his school life, he never forgot what he hoped to be.

When he was seventeen years of age, he asked the Provincial to receive him into the Franciscan Order. This pious priest thought that the boy was too young and not rugged enough for the austere life of a Franciscan. But when he heard that he was seventeen years of age, and had a true vocation, he accepted the young Majorcan.

After a most exemplary novitiate and a brilliant seminary course, Juniperro Serra was raised to the priesthood.

While still a young priest he obtained the degree of S.T. D. from the famous Lullian University, with an appointment to the John Scotus chair of philosophy, which position he held with distinguished success till he left Spain in 1749 for missionary work in Mexico.

After spending almost twenty years in the missions of Lower California and in the City of Mexico, Father Serra, and two other Franciscans, started out to evangelize the Indians of Upper California.

Like all such expeditions, the missionaries went under the protection of the Spanish soldiers. After landing in California a small temporary chapel was erected and dedicated, and the mission of San Diego was established.

Leaving there forty-six persons and three friars, the rest of the party started out to establish another mission at Monterey.

As they trudged along overland, they gave beautiful names of saints to the valleys, rivers, hills, and mountain peaks, many of which names survive to this day.

When they came to Monterey, they failed to recognize it, though they had on hand the minute description of Vizcaino and the Carmelites. So they pushed northward. In the course of their travels some of the soldiers happened to climb the hills back of the present City of San Francisco, and saw for the first time the beautiful bay. The vessel *San Jose* which was to meet them in Monterey, they hoped to see ill this expansive body of water.

Being disappointed, and running short of provisions, they were forced to return and reached Monterey by the end of November. For the second time, they failed to recognize it as the port they had set out to find and so they passed on, after having raised a cross on the shore with the inscription, "Dig at the foot and thou wilt find a writing."

They reached San Diego, January 24, 1770; but on their arrival when their report was made and compared with Vizcaino's description, it became eV1dent to them that they had been twice at Monterey and knew not the place.

Discouraged by the failure of this northern trip, by the hostile attitude of the Indians, and by the shortness of provisions, Portola decided to abandon Upper California if, by the end of March, a relief ship with stores and men did not arrive.

Great was the consternation of Father Serra and his brother Franciscans. They had come to stay; to do and die in the conversion of the Indians; and should the others go, they resolved to remain. Nevertheless they hoped that the project of the commander might not be carried out. So they betook themselves to prayer.

II

On the feast of St. Joseph, the nineteenth of March, the San Antonio sailed into the harbor with stores and reinforcements. All question of leaving was now given up, and it was decided to go once more to Monterey.

This time Father Serra accompanied the expeditionary corps which left San Diego in 1770 and arrived at its destination at the end of May.

On June 14, a humble chapel was dedicated to God under the invocation of San Carlos Borromeo. This mission afterward became the residence of the superior and the headquarters of all the other missions.

Encouraged by his good fortune thus far, Father Serra applied to the Mexican government for more helpers to establish other centers of missionary work. In answer to his appeal, ten Franciscans arrived in Monterey April 10, 1771.

In the year 1773, it was arranged that the missions of Lower California should be entrusted solely to the Dominicans, and those of Upper California to the 160 Franciscans. This arrangement gave the latter missionaries an opportunity to concentrate their forces. Thus they quickly produced the most remarkable effects in the conversion of the natives.

When the occupation of California was completed, there were four presidios or military stations - Santiago, Santa Barbara, Monterey, and San Francisco. The number of soldiers assigned to each was limited to two hundred and fifty, but they were rarely up to that number.

From these principal stations a guard of four or five was detached when required by the Fathers to accompany them on their journeys through the unoccupied portions of the country, and a detail of a few men was attached to each mission to preserve order and to defend the mission buildings and their inmates from the sudden attacks of the wild unconverted natives.

The pueblos or dwellings of the Indians were three in number, Los Angeles, San Jose, and Banciforte. They were served by the Fathers, though not subject to them in the sense tha t the missions were. Each pueblo was self-governing.

Within the missions only converted Indians resided under the immediate spiritual and temporal government of the Franciscans.

The buildings that went by the name of "mission" were quadrilateral, each side about 600 feet in length.

The whole consisted of a church, the quarters of the soldiers, the priest's convent, the school for boys and girls, and the storehouses.

The establishment was under the management of two religious, - one attended to the interior and the other to the exterior administration.

The female children, under the care of approved matrons, were taught the branches necessary for their condition of life; the more talented were trained in vocal and instrumental music.

The boys were taught mechanical and industrial trades. It goes without saying that all were taught the elementary three R's.

Morning and evening prayers said in common; and daily attendance at Mass gave to the life of the inmates a semi-monastic appearance.

Clustered around the mission buildings were the thatched huts in ·which lived the Indians converted to the faith. They tilled or used as pasturage the land about the mission for a distance of fifteen or twenty miles.

Father Serra founded the mission of San Antonio on July 14, 1771, and that of San Gabriel in August of the same year.

After having again asked by letter for more missionaries, he resolved to go in person to Mexico. On his way there, he founded the fifth mission at San Louis Obispo.

While in Mexico, Father Serra submitted to a Mexican commission the first official report of the Californian missions. From this we learn that the five missions already established were under the care of nineteen Franciscan missionaries.

The success of Father Serra's journey to Mexico proves that he was not only a zealous missionary and a saintly priest, but also a keen man of business and a firm advocate of the rights of the Church.

In 1773, Father Serra returned to Upper California accompanied by a number of extra soldiers and several additional Franciscans. As a consequence, new missions were established soon after at San Juan Capistrano, San Francisco, and Santa Clara.

Since it was very difficult for the Bishop of. Mexico to come to Upper California, Father Serra In 1778 received permission from the Pope to administer the Sacrament of Confirmation. During the greater part of the remainder of his missionary life, he was constantly traveling from mission to mission, confirming in all 5309 Indian converts.

The last hours of this worthy and zealous son of St. Francis were spent in making preparation for his approaching end. "Let me be laid in the church by the side of Father Crespi; afterwards when the new stone church is built, they may put me where they will." he said.

Seated in a chair, racked with pain, and without having slept for thirty-two hours, the dying missionary said to his companions: "Now I will sleep."

Then he walked to his bed made of two rough planks fastened together, lay down, placed his large wooden cross on his arms, and peacefully closed his eyes in the sleep of death.

This brief and imperfect sketch gives us an idea of some of the missionary work done in California by Father Juniperro Serra and his zealous and indefatigable Franciscan missionaries.

The esteem in which this heroic priest's memory is now held by the people of California, may be gathered from the facts that a non-Catholic lady has erected a granite monument to his honor in Monterey, and a beautiful bronze statue of gigantic size in Golden Gate Park, San Francisco, represents him as the" Apostolic Preacher." In 1884, the legislature of California passed a resolution making the 29th of August of that year, the centennial of Father Serra's burial, a legal holiday.

Song of the Swallows
By Leo Politi

At the foot of the low and soft hills near the sea lay the small village of Capistrano.

The bells of the mission church were ringing on that early morning of spring. Juan came running down the road through the village on his way to the little school near the mission. He ran through the gardens filled with flowers to the patio of the "sacred gardens." There he stopped to speak to old Julian.

Old Julian was the proud bell ringer of this beautiful mission. Many times had he told Juan the story of the mission, but always it seemed new.

"Long, long ago," Julian told him, "the good brothers of St. Francis came to this country from across the sea. Father Junipero Serra and the brothers walked along the wild trail through the wilderness. With the help of the Indians they built many mission churches."

"That is Father Junipero Serra," said Juan looking up at the statue in the garden. "He is my friend."

"The missions were like little villages," Julian said. "There the Indians learned to make shoes and harness, blankets and hats, tools and pottery-many of the things they needed in their daily life."

On his way to school and on his way home Juan liked to look at the flowers in the mission garden. They were so gay against the old walls!

Julian was also the gardener of the mission. He took much pride in showing Juan the plants, for he knew and loved each one of them.

Many birds came to the garden to nest, for here they were undisturbed. They flew happily among the trees and drank the fresh water of the old fountain. There were hummingbirds, white pigeons, sparrows, and other kinds of birds.

Julian always carried crumbs of hard bread in his pockets to feed them. The pigeons came and perched on his shoulders and on his hands.

But the most joyous birds were the swallows. There were hundreds of them nesting beneath the roof beams above the arches and their twittering filled the gardens with the sweetest music. They made spring a very happy time in Capistrano.

"Ever since I can remember," Julian told Juan, "the swallows have come in the spring on St. Joseph's Day and have gone away late in the summer."

"But how can little birds know when it is St. Joseph's Day?" Juan asked.

"That I do not know," said Julian.

Juan was full of curiosity about the swallows. He watched them build their small mud houses against the beams of the roof. The best time of all was when the old swallows taught the baby birds how to fly.

One morning Juan and Julian watched a family of young swallows seated in a row on an iron bar across the arch. One by one the old swallows gave them flying lessons.

At first, as the little birds tried to flutter, they were so clumsy and awkward! One of them tumbled to the ground.

"Poor little one!" cried Juan as he ran to pick him up.

He held the baby bird close and soothed him.

When they found he was not hurt, Julian set him back on the iron bar. The little swallow seemed eager to get back to his nest. Perhaps, he felt that it was feeding time.

One day late in the summer, Julian noticed that the swallows were noisier and more excited than usual. It seemed as if they were getting ready to leave.

"Juan!" he called. "The swallows are leaving us!"

Juan was sad because he knew he would miss them so much. He felt that he knew each one of them and they were like dear little friends to him.

The swallows rose, twittering, in the air, and flew toward the south. Juan and Julian watched, motionless, until they disappeared beyond the horizon.

Julian said, as he always did when the swallows left,
"Farewell little swallows,
For you we will yearn,
May God bless your journey
And guide your return."

"I shall pray for their return," said Juan. The swallows flew down the coastline.

"How wonderful the flight of the swallows is!" said Julian. "Just try to picture, Juan, the hundreds and thousands of miles they travel, high up in the air, looking down over strange and beautiful lands. I believe that, of all the creatures, God has given them the most freedom and happiness."

"But where are they going?" asked Juan.

"Some say to a land far south of us - some to a green island in the Pacific Ocean," said Julian.

"No one really can tell, but I do know, Juan, that they will go where there are flowers and fresh water streams and people who welcome and love them."

As the autumn and winter months set in, the colors in the mission gardens became quieter and softer. The mission was still lovely, but there was now a feeling of loneliness without the swallows.

On his way to school Juan often stopped and looked up with sadness at the empty nests. There the joyous swallows had lived and played, but now their little houses were still and lonely.

When the winter months were nearing an end, new buds began to swell and trees to bloom again. Soon the blossoming trees bent gently over the garden walks. They made lovely patterns against the sky and filled the clear air with fragrance. Juan felt he was going through an enchanted garden.

Julian worked hard in the gardens, for St. Joseph's Day was coming soon. He wanted the gardens to look their best for the swallows' return.

The sky was tinted red at early dawn on St. Joseph's Day. Soon the sun rose from behind the hills and cast a golden glow over the valley.

Juan and his friends came early that morning to greet the swallows. The boys wore their best suits and the girls, their newest dresses, with flowers and ribbons in their hair.

They played games, sang, danced, and acted little plays of olden days. As the happy fiesta went on, every now and then the children would look up at the sky.

Would the swallows come?

Hours of waiting and watching went by. Time dragged into the late afternoon with not a swallow in sight. The children became tired and discouraged. Some of them began to leave.

Then Juan, who was standing high up on the column of a broken arch near the edge of the playground, saw some little dots far off on the horizon.

"The swallows are coming!" he cried.

The children jumped up and down with joy

The little dots came nearer; they grew bigger and bigger. Soon hundreds of swallows circled over the mission. Juan ran and hugged Julian. "The swallows are here! I thought they would never come!"

"They came late, perhaps they met a storm on the way, but I told you, Juan, that they would return. See how glad they are!" said the wise old man.

The swallows were very much like little folks who had been on a long journey and were happy to be home again. They fluttered and twittered joyously and filled the gardens with sweet sound.

Juan and Julian went into the garden and rang the mission bells to tell the people of the valley that spring had now begun.

Roads Go Ever Ever On
By J.R.R. Tolkien

Roads go ever ever on,
Over rock and under tree ,
By caves where sun has never shone
By streams that never find the sea' ,
Over snow by winter sown,
And through the merry flowers of June
Over grass and over stone ,
And under the mountains in the moon.

Roads go ever ever on
Under cloud and under star ,
Yet feet that wandering have gone
Turn at last to home afar.
Eyes that fire and sword have seen
And horror in the halls of stone ,
Look at last on meadows green
And trees and hills they long have known.

Daniel Boone: This young man was one of the first Americans to cross the Appalachians. He crossed the mountains and saw the beautiful land of Kentucky. He knew it would be good for hunting, fishing, and farming. The trail he blazed was called **Wilderness Road.** In 1775, He led settlers through the Appalachian Mountains by way of the Cumberland Gap. The settlement he started in Kentucky was called Boonesborough. During the Revolutionary War, Boone fought the British-aided Indians on the south side of the Ohio River. After the War, the British agreed to give the United States this land known as the Northwest Territory.

In 1803, President Jefferson bought the **Louisiana territory** from the French. This land stretched from the Mississippi River to the Rocky Mountains. The

Louisiana Purchase doubled the size of the United States.

Hundreds of families moved west. They cleared the forest and prepared the land for farms. They raised corn, wheat, cattle, and hogs. They wanted to sell their extra crop, and used the Mississippi River to transport the goods. There were no good roads or railroads through the Appalachians yet. They put their crops on flatboats and floated them down the Ohio and Mississippi rivers.

Louis and Clark Expedition: President Jefferson wanted to know more about the land he bought from the French. Two men were hired to lead an exploration throughout the new land. They kept a journal of their 8,000 mile trip. They wrote descriptions of the landscape, minerals, wildlife, and Indians they had seen. They followed the Columbia River to its mouth in Oregon.

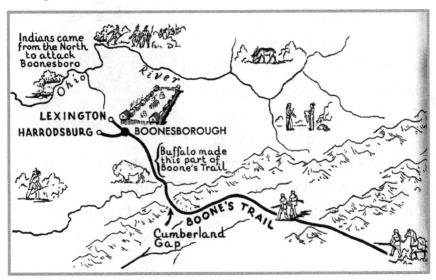

The Civil War

In **1619**, **slavery** began in our country in the settlement of Jamestown. The slaves, who were taken from their homes in Africa, were sold to work on the tobacco **plantations**. Slavery divided the country and led to a great war.

In the early **1800's** the United States was sharply divided on the question of slavery. There was much division and bitterness among the different states because of slavery. By **1850**, there were **15** states that allowed slavery, and **15** states that outlawed slavery.

The **16**th President of the United States of America was elected in **1860**, in the midst of this slavery conflict. His name was **Abraham Lincoln.**

He was a very talented and intelligent man, who also practiced virtue. He was a good leader for our country.

A month after Lincoln was elected, South Carolina declared that it was no longer part of the United States. Other states joined South Carolina and called their government the **Confederate States of America.**

Jefferson Davis was elected President of the Confederate States of America. He lived on a large plantation in Mississippi. He treated his slaves well and didn't believe the slavery was wrong.

Soon a war started between the United States and the Confederate States. This war was called the Civil War. The Civil War brought much destruction, death, and sadness to our country. Farms and houses were burned. Young men were killed in battle and wounded. Northern soldiers were called "boys in blue" because of the color of their uniform. They fought bravely to save the Union. The Southern soldiers fought hard and nobly for their native states. They were called Confederate soldiers.

Robert E. Lee: One of the greatest generals in the Confederate army. He was from the state of Virginia. He didn't think slavery was right and believed it to be a great evil. He thought it to be his duty to fight for his state. He resigned from the United States Army and joined the Confederacy. Honor and duty guided the southern general's decisions. He was brave and well-loved by his men.

In 1865, the Confederate armies surrender and General Lee surrenders to General Grant at Appomattox Court House.

Ulysses S. Grant: He was a great general for the Union army, fighting in the Upper Mississippi Valley. He was chosen by President Lincoln to be the commander in chief of all the Federal armies in the second half of the Civil War. Grant invaded the western Confederacy; he changed the course of the war by capturing Vicksburg, splitting the Confederacy in half. He was the first to fight General Lee well, pushing Lee south and forcing him to surrender. He allowed the southerners to surrender with honor. After the War, he became the 18th President of the United States of America.

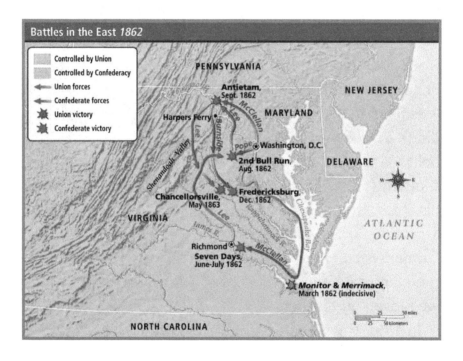

In the early days of our country, most Americans were **farmers**. In the beginning, almost all farm work was done by hand. It took a long time to cut wheat, and much grain was lost. In the 1800s, men invented a machine called a **reaper** that cut wheat quickly and evenly. Also, little grain was wasted.

Americans also made cloth from cotton in the **textile mills**. Turning cloth into clothing was hard and long work. In the 1800s, men also invented machines to do the sewing. This new invention was the sewing machine.

The first factories were run by **steam power**. The water needed to be boiled to produce the steam. First, men used wood for heating the water, but they soon found that **coal** made a much better fuel. There was much coal to be found in the United States.

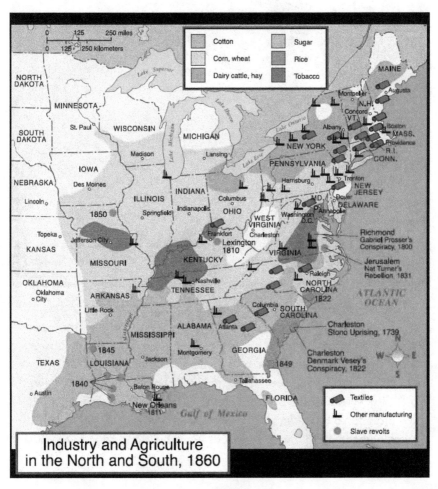

Industry and Agriculture
in the North and South, 1860

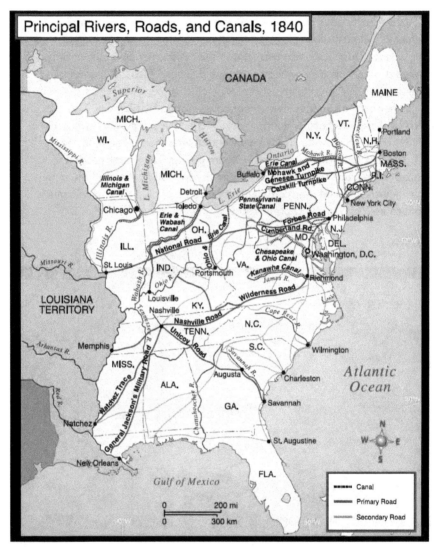

Principal Rivers, Roads, and Canals, 1840

The mayor of New York City had a great plan. He knew that many people were in the region around the Great Lakes. These people could sell grain, lumber, furs, and other raw goods to the eastern part of the United States and to Europe. The mayor's plan was to have an all-water route between the Great Lakes region and New York City, which would be from Hudson River to Lake Erie. Men dug a big ditch for a long canal. The **Erie Canal** was completed in 1825.

Beginning in 1828, many **railroads** were built and took away business from the canals.

Frederic Remington, "The Cowboy"

Frederic Remington,
"The Trooper"

Between 1843 and 1880, many Americans wanted to try farming in Oregon. They had heard of the wonderful land and wanted to make their home there. They traveled over the plains in covered wagons. This route is known as the **Oregon Trail**. It went from Independence, Missouri to Oregon. It was safer to travel in groups, so many families would make a party. They would select a captain and a scout to lead the way. On a good day, they would travel 15-20 miles, taking the group 5 or 6 months to complete their journey.

Dr. John McLoughlin: He was a Catholic doctor from Canada who decided that he loved the

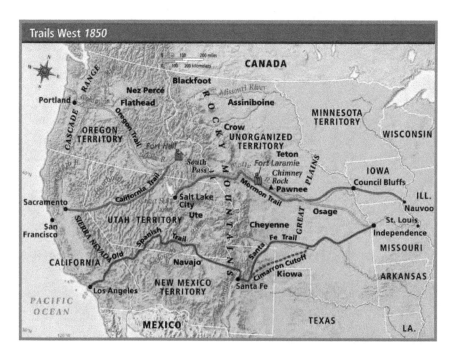

Trails West 1850

wilderness and fur-trading more than being a doctor. He lived at Fort Vancouver at the end of the Oregon Trail. He had made friends with the Indians in Oregon and greeted the new settlers as they arrived. Because he greatly helped the American settlers, he is called "the Father of Oregon." He helped many people and families with his works of charity.

Fr. Peter De Smet: He was a Jesuit priest from Belgium, who came to the United States for missionary work, particularly among the Indians. He is known as the "Apostle of the Rockies" because he worked with Indian tribes in the Rocky Mountain region. He also ministered to the people living in Oregon with Dr. McLoughlin. He built many missions in the west and helped establish peace, charity, and the Catholic Faith among the Indians.

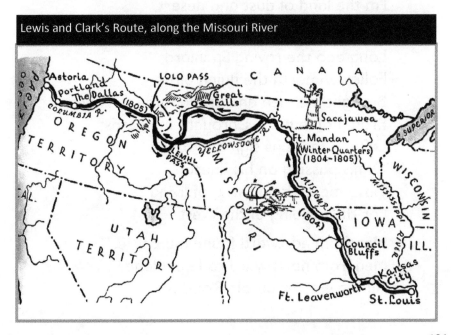

Lewis and Clark's Route, along the Missouri River

Cattle Country

by Mary Synon

I'm the land of wider ranges,
I'm the land of shorter grass,
I'm the country of the campfires
Where the great herds used to pass;
I'm the land of plain and mountain,
Land of mesa and of hill,
I'm the land of Heigh-ho Silver
And the land of Buffalo Bill.

I'm the land of ropes and saddles,
Clinking spurs and lariats whirled,
Cowboy chaps and wide sombreros,
I'm the rodeo of the world.
I'm the land of drives and roundups
Where the branding irons are pressed,
I'm the land of dust and desert,
I'm the wide and wondrous West.

Long ago the roving Spaniard
Followed north the flying birds,
Brought me men and brought me missions,
Brought me horses, brought me herds;
Left me these as sign and token
Of his passing on his quest,
Gave me faith and way of living
For the building of the West.

Men from eastward found my cattle,
Men from northward rode my land,
All the way to purple Rockies,

All the way to Rio Grande,
Rode my trails to every border,
Chisholm, Goodnight, Santa Fe,
Learned my ways and learned my language,
Strong and harsh and brave and gay.

Gone the wideness of my ranges,
Turned my older, brighter page,
But the cattle still are milling
Through the fields of purple sage.
Still the missions top the hillsides,
With the crosses on their spires,
Still the padres light the mesas
With the glow of holy fires.

I'm the land of toil and danger,
I'm the land of liberty,
I'm the old, old cattle country,
I'm the young land of the free,
I'm the land of dream and longing,
I'm the land of sun-baked sod,
But my Rockies touch the heavens,
And my trails lead up to God!

Among the great pioneers of America
Have been the Catholic missionaries;
And no one of them has been braver than

The Shepherd of Santa Fe

On a blazing hot day in August more than a hundred years ago, two weary men rode their weary horses up the Santa Fe Trail. Friends from their childhood, they had come a long way to this far Western mountain country. They had crossed an ocean and more than half a continent. They had suffered illnesses and shipwrecks. They had gone hungry and thirsty on this last, the most difficult part of their journey. They had escaped death by minutes.

Both of these brave men were French missionary priests. Both of them had labored in parishes in Ohio. Both of them lived only to love and serve God; and both of them would win fame as pioneer bishops of the great West.

One of them, John Lamy, was already the Bishop of Santa Fe. He had been made a bishop in Cincinnati and had set out for Santa Fe by way of New Orleans, since the season for travel on the overland trail was past. In New Orleans he found his sister ill in her convent. Because of this he missed the boat he was to take. He found passage on another, a miserable vessel which sank as it was reaching the Texas shore. Bishop Lamy saved only his life and his books.

He missed meeting his friend, Father Joseph, who was to go with him to Santa Fe. He left word that Father Joseph was to follow him and joined a group of soldiers. He was injured, and the soldiers had to go without him. Father Joseph overtook him, and together they joined another troop. The soldiers could go only part of the way with them, and the priests had to go on alone.

The journey was difficult and dangerous. The roads were poor. There was little water, and most of it was bad. There was no protection against enemy Indians or against white robbers, but they rode on and at last came in sight of Santa Fe.

The town, set high in the mountains of New Mexico, was the wildest town of a wild West. Crimes of·all sorts took place within it. Most of its people loved and feared God, but they also feared the gamblers, the robbers, and the murderers. Most of its people were Catholics, but there were few priests; and the Mexican bishop did not often come to Santa Fe. The people welcomed Bishop Lamy gladly.

Quietly Bishop Lamy set about making Santa Fe a better place. He gave out no orders, but he made men and women wish to make themselves better. In a little while the town began to show this spirit. His people began to help him as he helped them. He rebuilt churches that had fallen into decay. He built schools, a hospital, and an orphanage. He brought the Sisters 260 across the plains to help him care for children and the sick of the community.

He helped to build good roads. He asked the railroad company to employ native New Mexicans for its work in building new railroads. Knowing his love for them, his people gave him their love.

The governors of the territory became his grateful friends. The generals of the Army asked for and received his help. The great Army scout, Kit Carson, gave him loyal friendship. Only once did they disagree. That was the time when Carson favored the moving of the Navahoes by the government from their homes. Bishop Lamy felt that this was unjust. He was glad when the government moved the Indians back a few years later.

Arizona was added to his parishes. He made many and long journeys in order to meet and know his people. Often he had to ride on roads where every rock might be hiding an Indian warrior ready to kill a white man. He usually traveled alone, riding one horse, leading another. He carried his food with him hard-boiled eggs and crackers, for he did not like what; he called "the blessed bean" and "holy porridge."

Stories of the bishop's kindness are still told in Santa Fe. A Jewish merchant of the town was taken ill as he was returning with a wagon train. The leaders of the train forced him to leave his wagon; and, fearing that he had a deadly fever, they placed him in a trapper's sod house. They were leaving him, sick and alone, when Bishop Lamy passed by. Hearing the rumor about the sick man, he went to him and brought him to his wagon.

"I may have the fever," the merchant warned.

"We do not fear it," said the bishop. "We will take care of you."

In time Bishop Lamy became an archbishop. When he died, his body lay in the cathedral he had built.

Thousands of men and women looked for the last time
on the great archbishop who had been their guide,
their friend, their leader, the Shepherd of Santa Fe.

America the Beautiful

Katharine Lee Bates   Samuel A. Ward

2. O beautiful for pilgrim feet
Whose stern impassioned stress
A thoroughfare for freedom beat
Across the wilderness.
America! America!
God mend thine ev'ry flaw,
Confirm thy soul in self-control,
Thy liberty in law.

3. O beautiful for glorious tale
Of liberating strife,
When valiantly for man's avail
Men lavish precious life.
America! America!
May God thy gold refine
Till all success be nobleness
And ev'ry man divine.

4. O beautiful for patriot's dream
That sees beyond the years
Thine alabaster cities gleam
Undimmed by human tears.
America! America!
God shed His grace on thee,
And crown thy good with brotherhood
From sea to shining sea.

The bravest journeys across the Western plains
were those of the Indians
who walked three thousand miles
to bring a missionary back to their people.
It was no wonder that the priest
who went back with them
called these messengers

Bronze Angels

The Flatheads Seek a Blackrobe

Among the great tribes of the Northwest were the Flatheads. They were honest, wise, and kind far beyond the way of most of the tribes. Out in a lovely valley of the Rocky Mountains they lived in as much peace as their more warlike neighbors allowed them. For to the Flatheads - as to no other Indians of the Northwest - had come the Word of God.

The Word had come to them in a strange way. A little band of Catholic Iroquois - the Indians of the East - had left Canada and had moved to the West.

Their leader, Old Ignace, had been baptized and married in Canada. He and his family and their friends found their way to the Flatheads. They stayed with them and taught them what they knew of the Faith. Old Ignace became a great man among the Flatheads. He told the Indians of the West about the one true God. He taught them the truths of the Apostles' Creed. He taught them to make the Sign of the Cross and to say the Lord's Prayer. He told them of the Sacraments and of the Mass.

"How may we have all these things for ourselves?"

the Indians of the mountains asked the old man.

"Send for a Blackrobe," he told them over and over again. "Send for the priest who wears the black robe and who carries the Cross of Christ in his belt."

Morning and night the Flatheads said the prayers Old Ignace had taught them. They adored God. They kept Sundays holy. They baptized the dying and set crosses over their graves. They told other tribes of their Faith.

Within twenty years all the Indians of the neighboring valleys had joined the Flatheads in their prayers and in their wish for the coming of a priest.

How could they find a priest?

From the valley in the Rockies to the mission in eastern Canada was a journey of more than four thousand miles. A trader told them that there were Blackrobes in the city of the white men called St. Louis. That was only three thousand miles away!

To reach that city, the men of the Flatheads would have to cross high mountains, wide rivers, dry plains. They would be in danger of attack by their enemies.

"Shall we never see a Blackrobe?" asked the Flatheads.

At last Old Martin spoke. He was very old, the uncle of Old Ignace, and he too had known the priests of Canada.

"I will go to the city of the white men for the Blackrobe," he said.

With three other men he set out. No white man knew how they went, but at last they came to the city of St. Louis. There they found the priests whom the

Indians called the Blackrobes and told their story. One of the priests understood them. Someday, he said, a missionary would go to the mountains.

Old Martin and one of his friends died in the city of the white man. The other two Indians started back to the mountains, but they never reached them.

The Flatheads waited. Then, four years later, Old Ignace and his two sons set out. He too, with his sons, reached St. Louis. He too begged for a missionary.

Sadly Bishop Rosati had to tell him that there was no missionary who could go to his people.

"The world is so wide," the bishop said. "The work is so great, and the workers are so few."

The bishop promised that as soon as he could he would send a priest. He himself would soon go to Europe to find missionaries for the West.

Old Ignace went back to the Flatheads. For a long time they waited, but no priest came. Then, with four other Indians, he started again to St. Louis, the city by the rivers.

As they crossed the Sioux country, they met a band of three hundred Sioux warriors. Old Ignace was dressed as a white man. He could have escaped death, but he would not leave his friends. All five died. As they died, they asked God to let their deaths be sacrifices for their people.

A fur trader took the news of their death to the Flatheads. The Indians knelt for a long time in prayer. Then Young Ignace, son of Old Ignace, arose.

"I will go to the city," he said, "and I will bring back with me the priest who wears the black robe and carries the Cross of Christ in his belt."

"You cannot go alone:" said the old men of the tribe.

Another Flathead, Pierre, arose. "I too will go," he said.

"So be it," said the old men of the Flatheads and bowed their heads in prayer.

On the next day Young Ignace and Pierre set out on that journey of which the Great West still talks. They started alone, but, after a few days, they met a party of trappers and traveled with them for a few weeks.

Then, alone again, they crossed wide lands covered with low bushes until they came to the Missouri River. They went down the Missouri by canoe. Wild animals moved along the riverbanks. This was the country of the Sioux. Through every hour Young Ignace and Pierre were in danger of attack. They were hungry and thirsty. They suffered terrible heat by day and cold by night, but they kept on.

Pierre fell ill, and Young Ignace took care of him. Again they moved on.

They had started in April, and in the month of September they came to the Mission of St. Joseph, a wigwam on the banks of the Missouri River.

In that wigwam knelt a man who was to baptize thousands and thousands of Indians, who was to bring peace wherever he went. He was the noble priest who was to win the love of all men, white and red, whom he met through the long years of his mission.

He was the Apostle of the Rockies, Father Peter De Smet.

He arose from his knees as Young Ignace came into

the wigwam. Father De Smet had been ill, very ill. His black robe hung upon his big body. His eyes still shone with fever. But, when Young Ignace and Pierre, with tears in their eyes, begged him to go back with them, he made his promise.

"If God thinks me worthy, I will gladly give my life to help you," he said. "You are God's messengers," he told the Indians. He looked at their dark skins and added, "You are the bronze angels of God."

The Apostle of the Rockies

The next day Pierre started back to the Flatheads. He traveled alone, all alone, for three thousand miles between the Mission of St. Joseph to the country of the Flatheads.

Young Ignace went with Father De Smet to St. Louis, the city by the rivers. They joined their prayers that the priest might be sent back with the Indian. Then, in the next springtime, long before the covered wagons passed that way, Father De Smet and Young Ignace started out on the trail to the West.

They had seven horses, one for the priest, one for Young Ignace, and five for their baggage and food. For safety they joined a company of fur traders, although Father De Smet knew no fear.

"I thank God with my whole heart for having chosen me for this mission," he said. "Never have I been so happy."

They crossed dry plains and rode through deep valleys. After ten days the heat became terrible. Father De Smet fell ill with fever. The fur traders begged him to go back, but Father De Smet looked at Young

Ignace and saw sorrow in the Indian's eyes.

"No," he said, "I will go on."

He rode his horse until he was so weak that he could no longer sit on it. Then Young Ignace placed him on a sledlike platform made of logs and dragged by a horse. As the sled passed over the ruts in the rough trail, Father De Smet was shaken and jolted. His fever rose, and for three days he had only stale water to drink. Through all these hardships Father De Smet never complained.

Then for a few days the company moved across the green prairies. For the first time Father De Smet saw thousands of buffaloes and herds of deer. He saw wild flowers and the blue of the sky.

"God is good," he said, and grew better.

Again the country changed. The plains were dusty, the grass was burned, and the rivers were dry. Rocky cliffs began to rise about them. Among the rocks moved enemy Indians whose lands had been stolen by white men. Now they hated all white men.

On the last day of June the company saw a tiny settlement on the banks of a river. Every year the Indians of the northwest mountains came there to meet the traders and to sell skins of mink and beaver and fox.

As the weary travelers came near the settlement; Father De Smet saw many Indians. Not until a great company of them rode out to meet him did he know the Indians were expecting him.

The riders were the Flatheads. Pierre had brought them the priest's promise to come to them. 'The old chief had sent out scouts to find out if the Blackrobe and Young Ignace were with the company of traders. Then, with all his tribe, he had followed.

As they met, the Indians leaped from their horses. Father De Smet jumped down from his horse. The Flatheads moved around him, not as strangers, but as old friends.

They were like children welcoming their father who had been away for a long time. Father De Smet wept with joy as he put his arms around them. With tears in their eyes, they told him how they had fought a great battle to win their way to him.

"Our enemies attacked us," said the old chief, "but the Great Spirit had pity on us and helped us to clear all danger from the road you must follow."

Then began the hardest part of the journey. The road lay through the country of the most warlike tribe of Indians. With the Flatheads, Father De Smet crossed it safely, only to meet other Indian tribes who begged him to stay with them.

Father De Smet kept on with the Flatheads, and came, on the third of July, to the place where he said the first Mass ever to be said in the Rockies. He called the place the Plain of the Holy Sacrifice.

Through that summer the priest lived the life of an Indian. He ate roots or whatever game could be found. His bed was a buffalo hide. Wrapped in a blanket, he slept under the stars. In storms he had no shelter but a tiny tent.

For months Father De Smet was ill with the fever. Not until the time had come for his return to St. Louis did he grow better.

Long before sunrise of his last day among them, the Flatheads met to say good-by. No word of sorrow was spoken, but sadness filled all eyes.

"Why must you go?" the Indians asked him.

"I must go," said Father De Smet, "so that I may bring back more missionaries to the West."

"Will you come back?" the old chief asked.

"I will come back," the missionary promised.

He led the morning prayers while men and women sobbed. Then he spoke to them. "Love God," he said. "Serve God. Night and morning and every Sunday say your prayers together. Be good. Hurt no man. Will you all do this?"

"Yes, Father," they promised. Then they said good-by to him. "Safe journey," they said, one after another.

Then Old Big Face arose and said, "Blackrobe, may the Great Spirit go with you on your long and dangerous journey! Morning and night we will pray that you may reach your brothers in St. Louis.

"We will keep on praying until you come back to us, your children of the mountains. When the snows of winter have gone from the valleys, and when the first green of the springtime appears, our hearts, which are now sad, will once again be glad.

"As the prairie grass grows higher and higher in the springtime, we will go forth to meet you. Farewell, Blackrobe, farewell!"

For days men of the Flatheads rode with him to the east. Then, when they had come near the country of their enemies, the priest would let them go no farther.

"I shall be safe," he told them, "but you would not be safe. You must go back."

In the dawn of a Rocky Mountain morning he rode on to the east. The Indians held their horses on the hill until they could see him no more. The last one to turn away was Young Ignace.

"The Blackrobe has gone," he said. "He has gone, but he will come back. His God -our God- came back to life a little while after He had died to save us; and the Blackrobe, who is the messenger of God, will return."

That was more than a hundred years ago. Today, through all that land, rise the steeples of mission churches. For Father De Smet kept his promise and went back to the Flatheads. He brought other missionaries with him, and they, in turn, brought other missionaries, men who spoke the Word of God to white men and red men.

Today the buffaloes are gone. The Indians are nearly all gone. But the West is a great mission field-because once, long ago, Old Ignace, Pierre, and Young Ignace, the bronze angels of God, braved death and danger to bring the Gospel to their people.

Winslow Homer, "Song of the Lark"

Our God and Our Country

Long ago, God, our Father, created the rich gifts that make our country great.

In the dark earth He placed coal and oil by which we would be warmed. In the high heavens He created the sun, the moon, and the stars that would light our way. In the rich soil God placed growing plants by which we would be fed.

Long ago, God, our Father, blessed our land.

In the hearts of boys and girls He placed the gift of faith, by which they would believe in God and in their neighbor.

In the hearts of boys and girls He placed the gift of hope, by which they would put their trust in God.

To the hearts of all people He offers the gift of love, by which they can be true to one another.

God, our Father, made a plan for us in our country.

The people who fought to keep our country great knew God's plan. The people who suffered to keep our country blessed followed God's plan. We too must know and follow God's holy plan.

We must share the gifts that make our country great and blessed. We must obey the laws of home, school, Church, and State. We must love all people because they are children of God.

We, the children of America, must help to carryon God's plan for our great and blessed country.